BIG BOOK OF
WORD SEARCH

Andrews McMeel
Publishing

Kansas City • Sydney • London

Andrews McMeel Publishing, LLC
an Andrews McMeel Universal company
1130 Walnut Street, Kansas City, Missouri 64106

www.andrewsmcmeel.com

All puzzles supplied under license from Puzzler Media Ltd.
www.puzzler.com

14 15 16 17 18 PAH 10 9 8 7 6 5 4 3 2 1

ISBN: 978-1-4494-6487-5

Made by:
The P. A. Hutchison Company
Address and location of production:
400 Penn Avenue, Mayfield, PA 18433 USA
1st printing – 7/18/14

1
Superheroes and Villains

See if you can find all these characters in the grid, but be careful, because one of them can't be found.

AVENGERS
BATMAN
BLACK WIDOW
BLADE
BRUCE WAYNE
CAPTAIN AMERICA
CATWOMAN
CLARK KENT
DAREDEVIL
DOCTOR DOOM
FANTASTIC FOUR
FLASH GORDON
GHOST RIDER
GREEN GOBLIN
GREEN LANTERN
HAWKEYE
HULK
IRON MAN
LEX LUTHOR
LOIS LANE
LOKI
MR. FREEZE
PETER PARKER
PROFESSOR XAVIER
SILVER SURFER
SPIDER-MAN
SUPERMAN

```
J M I K O L R E K R A P R E T E P
S R R R Z S U P E R M A N Y Y S S
P F E E F A N T A S T I C F O U R
I R I K T G S B L A C K W I D O W
D E V O W T R Y T H V L E D A L B
E E A J C O I E A N I E G S U T C
R Z X E B I L W E V E H N N S A X
M E R H C N K V E N O K O G P T M
A I O T S E A D E S L D K T E H E
N S S G Y G E M T R R A A R T R N
U I S E R R N R O O I I N I A N S
E L E S A E I I G W N N N T I L Y
N V F D C D E H H A R A E U E L C
Y E O N E D S N M T M E G L E R E
A R R R A A T E G N P N D X I B N
W S P K L M R F O O E M L N S T A
E U H F L I T R U P B U A L O I L
C R G C C U I A E D T L S W O W S
U F T A I A H H B H L S I O S P I
R E A T C A T W O M A N I N H Y O
B R U M O O D R O T C O D C D L L
```

SWAMP THING   THOR   X-MEN
THE JOKER   WOLVERINE
THE PENGUIN   WONDER WOMAN

The missing character is _____!

2
God Bless ...

Can you find the American states listed below the grid?

```
B Z E E E T C N B K A N S A S T R T F S E
H H A A K S A L A E M O E R T B U E F T G
A R T R E G L H Y I R H U E D C A G L T R
W N T E I R I S S E O A L T I R E G O E F
A B A H E Z F S D R M D W T K O H S R S Y
I U C I O T O E L N R I C A R E S O I U K
I I T Y D U R N E C D E N G L L R G D H C
M N M S R N N H A E N S I N A E O U A C U
I L L I N O I S T N A A R N E L D E B A T
I L S A W O A E O S C D T R F S A N I S N
E S L O W G M C D N A L Y R A M O B H S E
T U R E N O M I S S I S S I P P I T A A K
I E B L O U I S I A N A S O R E T H A M U
O D A R O L O C L I G N M E M A I N E C A
```

ALABAMA	IDAHO	MINNESOTA
ALASKA	ILLINOIS	MISSISSIPPI
ARIZONA	INDIANA	MISSOURI
ARKANSAS	IOWA	
CALIFORNIA	KANSAS	
COLORADO	KENTUCKY	
CONNECTICUT	LOUISIANA	
DELAWARE	MAINE	
FLORIDA	MARYLAND	
GEORGIA	MASSACHUSETTS	
HAWAII	MICHIGAN	

3
...America

And here are the rest. See how quickly you can complete both puzzles.

MONTANA	OREGON	WEST VIRGINIA
NEBRASKA	PENNSYLVANIA	WISCONSIN
NEVADA	RHODE ISLAND	WYOMING
NEW HAMPSHIRE	SOUTH CAROLINA	
NEW JERSEY	SOUTH DAKOTA	
NEW MEXICO	TENNESSEE	
NEW YORK	TEXAS	
NORTH CAROLINA	UTAH	
NORTH DAKOTA	VERMONT	
OHIO	VIRGINIA	
OKLAHOMA	WASHINGTON	

```
O K L A H O M A B J P L U V I R G I N I A
D R P B T L K R O Y W E N T G R T I E P U
E C D E L O R I T E R E O I A L T G B E C
D W X R N D K A N I L O R A C H T U O S R
S A U I I N T A E W E S T V I R G I N I A
S S P H L A S R D Y A N H E I N H T S O T
Y H E S C L D Y E H O D C L E O R E G C G
M I I P S S M S L M T O A B A E U N T I N
R N E M A I R O R V R U R V B I L N P X I
S G E A C E D E N E A A O T E R A E I E M
E T S H J D V L G T S N L S G N M S T M O
U O A W R O E O I K A N I S N O C S I W Y
S N E E Y H N E A C D N N A A L R E T E W
P N I N E R N O R T H D A K O T A E A N B
```

4
Soccer Camp

See if you can find all the coaching words in the grid below. When you have found them all, write out the leftover letters from top to bottom in the spaces below the grid to spell out the punchline to the joke.

```
B I E C L O O H C S H E S R A E H E R A
T I N U S E X E R C I S E H F G U I D E
U M E D H E D T A U R U G G P O L I S H
O P E W O U C E C O E I A U N I C T E D
K R T E C C T N L E N N M O E N Y U O E
R O D A C L T E A S R A O R M C D L S D
O V T E L I S R T H S I A H E U U E S A
W E P I V N T R I T N P D T N L T A H R
R E R R U E U C E N E E R N T C S R C G
E D N O I C L R A R A A D U O A O N A P
A N C H T M I O P R I T S R R T S U O U
R E R U T C E L P N P P E R F E C T C B
```

COACH	GUIDE	MASTER	RUN THROUGH
COUNSELOR	GURU	MENTOR	SCHOOL
DEVELOP	HONE	PERFECT	STUDY
DIRECT	IMPROVE	POLISH	TEACH
DRILL	INCULCATE	PRACTICE	TRAIN
EDUCATE	INDOCTRINATE	PREPARE	UPGRADE
ENHANCE	INSTRUCT	PRIME	WORK OUT
EXERCISE	LEARN	REAR	
FOCUS	LECTURER	REHEARSE	

Why did the manager flood the soccer pitch?

_____ ___ _____ ___ _____

___ ____ ____!

5
Solar System

Have a go at finding all of these space-related words in the grid.

ASTEROID
CALLISTO
CERES
CRESSIDA
DIONE
DYSNOMIA
EARTH
ENCELADUS
ERIS
EUROPA
GANYMEDE
GAS GIANT
HAUMEA
HYPERION
JUNO
JUPITER
LUNAR CYCLE
MAKEMAKE
MARS
MERCURY
NEPTUNE
NEW MOON
ORBIT
PALLAS
PLANET
PLUTOID
SATURN

SOLAR FLARE
SOLAR WIND
SPACE
SUNSPOT
TETHYS

TITAN
TRITON
VENUS
VESTA

```
M E R I S E A D I S S E R C B E
P E R N C S F N B C O G D F N O
A H R A R B O G O N E I K U O R
L W P C L U H L U I O R T G T B
L S F B U F T J A N R P E N I I
A H H I O R R A E R E E E S R T
S N A T I T Y A S N W W P V T M
L U N A R C Y C L E M I L Y A I
O C D S E A L V P O G I N K H K
E O H Y D O E E O L S R E D B A
N T I H E L W N O E U M C D I A
C S T T M H A U M E A T R M S S
E I F E Y A N S I K E E O T L U
L L O T N M G H E N T N E I A N
A L T N A I G S A G S R R E D S
D A N R G I E L O Y O C D A L P
U C S R T N P I D I V E S T A O
S J U P I T E R D A P O R U E T
```

6
Watch the Birdie

Can you find all the listed birds in the grid below?

```
N J B L A C K B I R D S C Y W Y T T L W K
G I M T I B H Y H T P N E O R O S E L A I
N Y U W I W A C D A T M A A N A R S U D N
I E I G R F I L R R E H N C L D W C G E G
L K S E N R I R D N I A O B U I O T A R F
R R N T T E O E A E C B A J F O N R E S I
A U V S N W P W E L A T G T A A T M S W S
T T O I S O S T Y W R G E N S C A N M A H
S R E K C E P D O O W I L A I C K S H L E
E O C D U C K H S F T N E E A M E D I L R
L P R D O V E S A S O H E W D T M F A O N
I W A R B L E R E W P E S L O M H U T W U
R E N E S O O G M N K P E L I C A N H I S
Y E E E R U T L U V O D N O E G I P A L R
```

ALBATROSS	EMU	OSTRICH	SWAN
BALD EAGLE	FOWL	PELICAN	SWIFT
BLACKBIRD	GOOSE	PENGUIN	TOUCAN
CANARY	HAWK	PHEASANT	TURKEY
CONDOR	HUMMINGBIRD	PIGEON	VULTURE
CRANE	JACKDAW	SEAGULL	WADER
CROW	KINGFISHER	SPARROW	WARBLER
DOVE	KIWI	STARLING	WOODPECKER
DUCK	MACAW	SWALLOW	WREN

7
It's about Time

See if you can find all the time-related words in the grid. But be careful, because one of the listed words does not appear in the grid.

ANNUAL
DECADE
FORTNIGHT
FUTURE
HOUR
INSTANT
JIFFY
LATER
MINUTE
MOMENT
MONTH
NOW
ONCE
PAST
PERIOD
PRESENT
QUARTER
SEASON
SECOND
SPELL
STAGE
TERM
WEEK
YEAR
YESTERDAY

```
K J D N O C E S Q I L G T C I
L R H I C J I F F Y M L N F G
W I E A E S O L R O I L A U H
A E S T O G L S M C Y D T T R
I A E L R E A E E A G S S U K
L O R K P A N T D A I A N R M
A P P S W T U R S H S Y I E I
U C R D L D E Q S R A O R O N
N I A E E T R S E O I E N L U
N G M C S T H G I N T R O F T
A A A E H E E C D A E N R H E
S D Y U O I N O L T E C P A L
E N R E U I S T E O A T N W Y
E C D L R P E R I O D C R O G
N M O N T H M M I T S A P N S
```

The word that does not appear in the grid is _____!

8
Healthy Living

See how quickly you can find all the words listed below the grid.

```
O B Z X O O O H R G N S O D R N S O B R H
N S O T I F N U C D R G Y T M I N S O T R
I E L H U N S E O C D U S E C I T C A R P
Y P R T I N A B E L N A M G N M S O R T G
T I A A E H I N U S F E U C D L N S R A A
R O I S T E A A K R S E L O I D E L M T G
O G M A T E B I R E C D C N R R X E H N A
P W E A K I L S U T I I O A T E E P A U W
S L N R E L M B I S N P W O A T R E C F K
Y D L R E E G E E E N K L M I S C A H E Y
O Z U D L T R N P E W E A A B I I L P S O
E C A D D T R T F A F A N I Y E S S L O G
M H I L T U A H E A L T H Y R E E N I S E
```

AWKWARD	FEEBLE	TRAIN
CLUMSY	FUN	UNFIT
EXERCISE	GAME	UNSKILLED
FAST	GAWKY	WEAK
	HEALTHY	
	IDLE	
	INEPT	
	LAZY	
	PASTIME	
	PLAY	
	PRACTICE	
	SPORTY	

9
Something Fishy

Find all of these tropical fish-related words in the grid. Once you've done that, write out the leftover letters from top to bottom to spell out the joke below the grid.

ALGAE
ANGELFISH
AQUARIUM
AQUATIC PLANT
BLACK MOLLY
CICHLID
CLOWN LOACH
CLOWNFISH
CORYDORAS
DANIO
ELECTRIC EEL
FLYING FOX
GILLS
GOLDFISH
GRAVEL
HEATING
JACK DEMPSEY
LIGHTING
MINNOW
NEON TETRA
RAINBOWFISH

RASBORA
RED ZEBRA
ROCKERY

SCALES
SUBSTRATE
SWORDTAIL

TIGER BARB
TROPICAL
WATER

```
L I A T D R O W S B A R O B S A R
F N W H H T S A R T Q D O S Q H G
L E E A S E R A M A U O N U Y S I
Y E S O L I B O N T A E A R R I L
I S E A N R F G P C T R E Y E F L
N R C C E T E N L I I K E L E D S
G S E G I L E O W U C S D I T L A
F N I D F R W T M O P A I G A O R
O T I I Z N T I R M L A L H R G O
X I S T L E N C E A A C H T T R D
E H N O A N B D E T N F C I S A Y
I A A A O E K R S L T H I N B V R
A C G W D C H W A T E R C G U E O
H N B L A C K M O L L Y D S S L C
H I P J A S H S I F W O B N I A R
```

_ _ _ _ _   _ _   _ _ _   _ _ _ _ _ _ _ _ _

_ _ _ ?

_ _ _ _ _   _ _ _   _ _ _ _ _ !

10
Around Paris

See if you can find all of
these words in the grid.
We've put one in to help
get you started. One of
the words can be found
three times—can you
spot which one it is?

ARC DE TRIOMPHE
BISTRO
CAFE
CHAMPS ELYSEES
EIFFEL TOWER
ELYSEE PALACE
ETOILE
FOLIES BERGERE
FRANCE
GLASS PYRAMID
LATIN QUARTER
LOUVRE
METRO
MONA LISA
~~PARIS~~
CENTRE POMPIDOU
SEINE
SORBONNE

French...

Can you spot all of these words related to France in the top grid?

AU REVOIR	GARLIC
BAGUETTE	GOURMET
BERET	LOUVRE
BONJOUR	MADAME
CHAMPAGNE	MERCI
CHATEAU	MONSIEUR
CHEESE	SEINE
CREPE	TRUFFLE
CROISSANT	VINEYARD
ESCARGOT	WINE

```
Y W E S C A R G O T A
B J E R E U D V L L U
S A E N O I I H O L R
T P G J G N N E U U E
E E N U E A L E V A V
B O M Y E F P M R E O
B E A R F T E M E T I
S R R U U R T N A A R
D P R E C O I E D H S
L T H I T W G I N C C
T N A S S I O R C S Y
D L I N N G A R L I C
P S O O T C H E E S E
F I L M E M A D A M H
```

...Fries

See if you can find all of these fried foods in the bottom grid.

BACON	HAMBURGER
BANANA	HASH BROWNS
BREAD	MUSHROOMS
CHICKEN	ONIONS
CHIPS	SAUSAGE
EGGS	STEAK
FISH	TOFU
FRITTERS	TOMATOES

```
D P W D H S I F T I N
E P B E B D T O F U E
H I A N E R M T R I K
A E C N S A E T E S C
M S O C T P D A R A I
B R N O S I I E D N H
U N E W S A T H S A C
R S E G O T U T C N P
G O G T I R E S H A R
E E I R E A B U A B A
R N F E K O C H D G R
M U S H R O O M S T E
I A E S N O I N O A G
N M K O R T I A E P H
```

13
Horsing Around

If you are keen on horses, this puzzle is for you. Find all the listed breeds of horse in the grid below. When you have found all the words, write out the leftover letters from top to bottom in the spaces below, to spell out a joke about horses and its punchline.

```
H O L S T E I N E R W R W N H T Y E R E S
N T D S O R R A I A K E E O A A A E P H U O
O R C R S H E S R R E L G N B I E R F O W
D A L H E A K M A S I O A D A R B F S A N
N K Y U T F B N S S S N D C Z O A L K C
A E D H S L R E A T O A H H R L Z L R A I
I H E N O I N E F B L O E D K U E I M A D
S N S O A N T R K E S R L P R B B A P G N
S E D E E G I A V I O T U A A A R E I I A
U R A T Y E R E N N R N R L P G U D R A L
R R L E S R L O I O C O A U U P R G L L E
H O E E R C S E M H P F N E P A A I H T C
F R I E S I A N A I R E V O N A H A L T I
```

APPALOOSA	GIDRAN	KNABSTRUP	RUSSIAN DON
ARABIAN	HAFLINGER	LIPIZZANER	SORRAIA
CAMARGUE	HANOVERIAN	LUSITANO	SUFFOLK PUNCH
CLEVELAND BAY	HOLSTEINER	MORGAN	TENNESSEE
CLYDESDALE	ICELANDIC	NORIKER	TERSK
FALABELLA	IRISH DRAUGHT	OSTFRIESE	TRAKEHNER
FRIESIAN	KLADRUBER	PERCHERON	WARMBLOOD

_____ __ _____ __ _____

_____ ___ ____? _____!

14
Up, Up, and Away

All the words in the list start with the letters UP.
How quickly can you find them all?

UPBEAT
UPCOMING
UPDATE
UPENDING
UPGRADES
UPHEAVAL
UPHELD
UPHILL
UPHOLD
UPKEEP
UPLAND
UPLIFTED
UPMARKET
UPPERCUT
UPLOAD
UPPERS
UPRIGHT
UPRISING
UPROAR
UPROOTED
UPSCALE
UPSETS
UPSHOT
UPSIDE
UPSTAGED
UPSTAIRS
UPSTART

```
E E M I T P U U B F U P T U R N E D
T V U C B P C G P N O F M N O C I U
A U U P L B N N M H S A D A O L P U
D O C A S I I U N C E E L O I S N N
P A N R S E P O I R S L D L T W M P
U D F I E E T U T A R B D A O E C E
N P R I N P P S O E I V R T R A L E
N P R D R R P E I S A T P U U G U K
U U I O O U T U U O T U A P P E P P
E N P A O H C U P L S L R C W N S U
G K R M G T P M S A P L I O A S T G
A K A I A B E H C V U E L M R O A N
R N R T E R E D A A U P S I D E G I
A P B A P I K L L E S W O N H E E W
U C T D R U F E E H A N I G E P D S
S U P P E R S L T P T H G I T P U P
O D E T F I L P U U M D L O H P U U
H A U P S U R G E R E U P S H O T N
```

UPSTREAM   UPTOWN
UPSURGE   UPTURNED
UPSWING   UPWARD
UPTAKE
UPTIGHT
UPTIME

Blooming Marvelous

See how quickly you can find all the listed flowers in the grid. But be careful: one of the flowers can be found twice.

ANEMONE
BEGONIA
BLUEBELL
BUTTERCUP
CARNATION
CROCUS
DAFFODIL
DAISY
FOXGLOVE
GARDENIA
GERANIUM
HYACINTH
IRIS
JASMINE
LILAC
LOTUS
LUPIN
MAGNOLIA
MARIGOLD
ORCHID
PANSY
PETUNIA
POPPY

PRIMROSE
SNOWDROP
SUNFLOWER
TULIP
VIOLA

M	A	R	I	G	O	L	D	J	A	I	N	O	G	E	B	X
H	T	E	H	C	O	T	G	A	R	D	E	N	I	A	E	E
T	Y	E	N	R	A	H	S	E	E	A	S	R	T	N	G	C
M	E	A	C	O	A	L	L	S	W	I	R	I	O	E	T	R
E	A	H	C	L	M	I	I	W	O	S	H	I	R	E	D	O
S	I	G	O	I	D	E	F	L	L	Y	T	A	R	I	T	C
D	E	I	N	O	N	O	N	R	F	A	N	I	P	U	L	U
S	V	L	F	O	X	T	E	A	N	I	T	P	I	B	S	S
E	C	F	L	G	L	D	H	R	U	N	E	R	L	R	N	H
P	A	S	L	E	T	I	A	M	S	L	N	I	U	E	O	V
D	O	O	N	R	B	C	A	E	O	S	I	M	T	A	W	Y
T	V	P	U	C	R	E	T	T	U	B	M	R	Y	E	D	S
E	C	D	P	R	G	N	U	M	S	A	S	O	H	E	R	N
T	R	N	E	Y	A	S	B	L	S	W	A	S	E	C	O	A
D	T	P	E	T	U	N	I	A	B	R	J	E	F	A	P	P

The flower that can be found twice is

_____!

16
Animal Jumble

Let's see how good you are at finding animals and how quickly can you spot them all in the grid.

ALLIGATOR
BADGER
BEAR
BEAVER
BUFFALO
CAMEL
CAT
CHAMELEON
CHEETAH
CHIMPANZEE
COW
CROCODILE
DEER
DOG
FROG
GAZELLE
GIRAFFE
GOAT
GORILLA
HAMSTER
HEDGEHOG
HIPPOPOTAMUS
HORSE
LION
LIZARD
LLAMA
MONKEY

MOOSE
MOUSE
PANDA
PANTHER
PIG

RABBIT
RAT
RHINOCEROS
SHEEP
SQUIRREL

TIGER
TOAD
TORTOISE
WOLF
ZEBRA

```
Y K V R H I N O C E R O S Q N Y N
P A D N A P U N S G O H E G D E H
H E N S S K G S W R G T N R Y O U
T O E N U S I O O O A O T E D W G
R C R H N M S T R C U R I H T O L
E O V S S N A I L F I T S T T L E
G W Y D E G L T I N I O S N K F M
I C U T I L N I O S W I E A C M A
T D H L A T N I N P E S S P O T C
S R L I B U F F A L O E U N E R N
Q A I Y M R E E D S E P K C E D Z
U E A R T P L N C I C E P G E E A
I B F S E L A R E H Y T D I B L G
R L U F E S I N A N E A A R H I R
R A T Z A E U M Z C B E A D P D A
E T A S V R E O K E S R T G T O B
L G O I A L I E M O E N O A L C B
R E V A E B S G O L L A M A H O I
R E P O D A W M R E T S M A H R T
T I N N Y U L I Z A R D E C D C L
```

17
The Sound of Music

Have you ever seen this fantastic film? Well, if you have then you will have no problem finding all the listed words to finish the wordsearch.

ABBEY
ALLELUIA
ALPS
AUSTRIA
BRIGITTA
CAPTAIN
CONVENT
DO-RE-MI
EDELWEISS
FRANZ
FRAU SCHMIDT
FRIEDRICH
GERMAN
GOVERNESS
GRETL
HAMMERSTEIN
HERR ZELLER
JULIE ANDREWS
KURT
LAKE
LIESL
LOUISA
MARIA
MARTA

J	D	N	A	L	R	E	Z	T	I	W	S	O	N	G	X
G	H	E	R	R	Z	E	L	L	E	R	T	M	I	Y	S
E	N	I	A	T	P	A	C	A	C	R	N	A	A	K	A
R	Y	C	A	B	B	E	Y	A	K	M	E	X	T	O	L
M	O	S	C	J	R	H	I	O	Y	E	V	D	N	O	Z
A	A	Y	S	O	U	R	C	H	D	N	N	E	U	K	B
N	H	L	L	E	A	L	G	O	T	N	O	T	O	B	U
I	T	F	P	M	N	N	I	D	E	P	C	W	M	B	R
E	E	D	S	S	I	R	O	E	O	D	P	E	R	C	G
T	A	D	I	N	F	R	E	A	A	R	U	I	T	F	N
S	S	U	R	M	E	R	I	V	O	N	G	L	O	G	P
R	L	O	S	M	H	U	I	C	O	I	D	E	E	P	H
E	M	T	I	T	L	C	E	E	T	G	T	R	A	R	N
M	A	I	E	E	R	S	S	T	D	S	Y	R	E	O	P
M	T	C	L	R	S	I	A	U	D	R	T	T	P	W	N
A	R	L	I	I	G	E	A	B	A	N	I	W	S	L	S
H	A	L	O	U	I	S	A	O	O	R	A	C	E	I	T
T	M	N	Z	N	A	R	F	V	H	R	F	U	H	E	R
I	A	G	N	T	H	E	B	A	R	O	N	E	S	S	U
L	E	C	D	S	S	S	I	E	W	L	E	D	E	L	K

MAX DETWEILER
MORNING HYMN
MOUNTAIN

PRELUDE
PROCESSIONAL
ROLFE

SALZBURG
SONG
SWITZERLAND

THE BARONESS
VON TRAPP
WAR

18
Canned Foods

Try to find all these canned products.

```
Y K W I L O I V A R Y K S M U L P W Y S G
L F L C C D I C E D P O T A T O E S P E T
P I Y U D O L G K H O S S T Y R T N I N V
E I A S L W R O D T R E L A B O R F N I S
A N I T E L O N G I P I M L R A H T E D M
R S B A K E D B E A N S C R A R R N A R O
H N E R N C I Y H D P O A E E B N C P A O
A A S D O D O S L A B C R N P A T R P S R
L E A C T T A C G N I E R A S U T A L E H
V B E O H T A H T R E O E A C O D T E M S
E R P E S I E P N I C H U F M A L D A M U
S E I A C T L O I T U S G A N E M H I D M
S N P T T U M I E O A R T K V O R T I N E
P N U I U L A E N G C O F P E A C H E S G
A U O F A N W S E S N A E B N E E R G L R
M R S S E S A G N I L L I F E I P E A R S
```

BAKED BEANS	HAM	PIE FILLING	SOUP
CARROTS	MACARONI	PINEAPPLE	SPAGHETTI
CHILI	MEATBALLS	PLUMS	SPAM
CORNED BEEF	MUSHROOMS	RAVIOLI	SWEET CORN
CRAB	PASTA SHAPES	RICE PUDDING	TAPIOCA
CUSTARD	PEACHES	RUNNER BEANS	TOMATO
DICED POTATOES	PEAR HALVES	SALMON	TUNA
FRUIT COCKTAIL	PEARS	SARDINES	VIENNA SAUSAGE
GREEN BEANS	PEAS	SAUCE	YAMS

19
Eat Your Greens

All of these vegetables can be found on the grid.

ARTICHOKE
ASPARAGUS
AVOCADO
BEANS
BEETROOT
BOK CHOY
BROCCOLI
CABBAGE
CAULIFLOWER
CELERIAC
CELERY
CHARD
CHICKPEA
CHICORY
CUCUMBER
KALE
LEEK
LENTILS
LETTUCE
MIZUNA
ONION
PARSNIP

```
F V A N U Z I M A S P A R A G U S
N Q D C D G F D O D A C O V A N C
A S S H A L L O T G D N G M A H U
E S W H S I D A R F L D Y E I N C
B V P E T N R I S E S O B C Y R U
A D L I E U G E E P H Q K N O M M
E Y A M N T N K L C R P U C C E B
S I T N E A C A K E E O K A L I E
L Y W O K D C O E A C E U T S F R
N P R I O S B H R P T L S T L H A
B E G O H R S M R N I I C N S I G
R P P Y C L T S E F H Y H D P L A
O P R O I I P E L T L R A N I I B
C E E T T A H O E I E E R E N S A
C R N L R A W C O B T L D I R R T
O E E S A E T T L I T E H G U N U
L M N E R K D O S V U C O R T T R
I I S A E P S S E R C R E T A W I
P E N I K P M U P U E N O N I O N
C A B B A G E F Z L S T O M A T O
```

PEANUT	RADISH	SPINACH	TOMATO
PEAS	ROCKET	SPROUTS	TURNIP
PEPPER	RUTABAGA	SQUASH	WATERCRESS
POTATO	SEA BEAN	SWEET CORN	YAM
PUMPKIN	SHALLOT	THISTLE	ZUCCHINI

20
Butterflies

Look for all of the listed butterflies. Be careful, though, one of them cannot be found in the grid.

APOLLO   COMMA   RED ADMIRAL
BRIMSTONE   DUKE OF BURGUNDY   RINGLET
CABBAGE WHITE   GRAYLING   SKIPPER
CAMBERWELL BEAUTY   HEATH FRITILLARY   WOOD WHITE
CLOUDED YELLOW   ~~PEACOCK~~

```
H O S                                       S D N
R E L C                                  S U K N
S I A L L                                T K C C N
S T N T O O                            R E O A I E
E A N G H P U                        S O C B A N T
E R M M L F A D                    I F A B E O N E
C A M B E R W E L L B E A U T Y A
S O S T I T D U P G R S I
F K I C E H T R Y E A M N H S
G N I L Y A R G I W E I E D W R T
I A P E G N U M H L R L S O D R T
I P A E N P I   B L H L N O U
E E C D D T     S A R O O A
R Y O E         I R T W
E N A           R Y S
```

The butterfly that cannot be found in the grid is _____!

Indoor Games

Can you find all the listed indoor games in the grid?

```
H S O E F V Z T T E N P I N B O W L I N G
U Y Q N L F R M R R H B O G G L E D E W E
N A R E T T S N O I T S E U Q Y T N E W T
G S E R E H T R L M V Y I N F A E A M D T
R N R L U E E O V A R I A F L R Y L O L I
Y O E I B K A D B R E M A D O A L Y N I C
H M R G O B M I O E G S A L H G K D O A T
I I E O D O A S U N H R N T P E A N P T A
P S N A I L S R A W K T Z I O U E A O E C
P S R E K C E H C E S E N I H C R C L H T
O T C D R F A N I S E B Y I E S L S Y T O
S O G M U A R E N I A S E O P C D A U N E
C H U T E S A N D L A D D E R S L R T I P
N I S R I A H C L A C I S U M E A S B P T
```

BOGGLE

CANDY LAND

CHINESE CHECKERS

CHUTES AND LADDERS

DARTS

GO FISH

HANGMAN

HUNGRY HIPPOS

MONOPOLY

MUSICAL CHAIRS

PINBALL

PIN THE TAIL ON THE DONKEY

SCRABBLE

SIMON SAYS

SNOOKER

SORRY

SPIN THE BOTTLE

TENPIN BOWLING

TIC-TAC-TOE

TRIVIAL PURSUIT

TWENTY QUESTIONS

YAHTZEE

22
My, My, My

All the words listed below have something in common: they end with the letters MY.
How quickly can you find them all?

ACADEMY
ALCHEMY
ANATOMY
ASTRONOMY
BALMY
BARMY
BIGAMY
CHUMMY
CLAMMY
CREAMY
DREAMY
DUMMY
ECONOMY
ENEMY
FILMY
FOAMY
GLOOMY
GRIMY
INFAMY
JAMMY
MONOGAMY
MUMMY
PLUMMY
PYGMY
ROOMY
SCRUMMY
SHAMMY

W	J	X	Q	E	T	P	M	E	N	C	H	U	M	M	Y
E	Y	M	O	N	O	C	E	O	P	T	Y	I	E	S	J
N	T	B	A	L	M	Y	E	L	N	M	D	I	N	Q	A
Y	Y	G	E	P	S	T	U	I	R	O	E	L	N	U	M
S	M	R	P	E	C	M	D	E	R	Y	G	T	I	I	M
B	M	I	E	Y	M	L	D	S	Y	N	M	A	S	R	Y
R	A	M	L	Y	G	I	T	H	M	I	E	R	M	M	P
I	H	Y	W	S	X	M	H	I	M	N	E	C	O	Y	D
N	W	L	S	A	R	I	Y	M	A	O	F	O	T	T	E
F	N	R	T	S	E	M	O	M	L	A	R	A	I	L	S
A	T	G	F	B	A	Y	E	Y	C	C	L	D	N	R	H
M	Y	S	I	G	G	O	M	A	S	C	R	U	M	M	Y
Y	T	M	I	E	D	L	D	O	H	Y	M	M	A	H	S
M	P	B	M	U	Y	E	O	E	N	Y	L	N	R	E	Y
M	I	E	M	U	M	M	M	O	S	O	U	O	T	C	M
U	D	M	L	Y	T	Y	A	R	M	G	R	M	N	Y	O
M	Y	D	R	E	A	M	Y	E	I	Y	S	T	M	A	T
Y	M	R	A	M	S	L	Y	M	R	A	B	E	S	Y	A
H	E	O	T	R	N	I	E	A	B	C	N	I	L	A	N
P	S	W	O	E	C	F	D	T	R	E	F	A	N	I	A

SHIMMY   SQUIRMY   TUMMY
SLIMY   STORMY   YUMMY
SMARMY   TAXIDERMY   WHAMMY

Toy...

See if you can find all of these toys and games in the top grid.

BALL
DOLL
DOMINOES
FRISBEE
JIGSAW
KITE
LEGO
MARBLES
PARCHEESI

PUZZLE
ROBOT
SCOOTER
SKATEBOARD
SKATES
SLINKY
TEDDY BEAR
TRAIN SET
YO-YO

```
H U F W J N T C N H U
S K A T E B O A R D G
I O G E L N B K I T E
M S R E T O O C S O P
C N E H U L R I Y N K
A F C E L R J O T G R
S M R A H I Y R I A M
E N B I G C A A E S A
O P P S S I R B T L R
N L A U N B Y A R I B
I W L S Z D E F P N L
M I E O D Z E E H K E
O T U E D A L N E Y S
D O T S K A T E S C D
```

...Story

Can you find all of these things you can read in the bottom grid?

ANNUAL
ARTICLE
BOOKLET
COMIC
DIARY
ESSAY
GUIDE
JOTTER
JOURNAL

LEAFLET
LEDGER
LETTER
MAGAZINE
NEWSPAPER
NOVEL
PAMPHLET
STORYBOOK
THRILLER

```
N E W S P A P E R F L
A R W V B Z S H S A A
N E C D I O R N R S N
N T K B Y E O T H M R
U T U O G R I K A I U
A O C D O C A G L T O
L J E O L B A I E E J
E L N E M Z Y L D Y T
A S C D I I H R A G M
F E I N N P C S O S F
L D E I M H S U A T N
E I S A L E T T E R S
T U P L E V O N O C D
R G I R E L L I R H T
```

25
Red...

Here are a list of things connected to the color red.
Can you spot them all in the grid?

```
Y M R U B Y T O O R T E E B W C O R A L V
R X A S N A F T D R C S S N O S M I R C D
R N S R N A E I O K L F U C H S I A C W A
E D O N O N I U R S A S H L W F A R D T H
B R E I R O G T M E R S E S D I A V N A L
L H L A L E N U I L E N E R U N N E I P I
U U G B S I L A O T T N I T B L G E E U P
M B D L E P M B G N I B G E X A B S R H S
E A A K H G S R T E Y O R I M O T N A C T
S R E M E T O O E D A R I L N S B W D T I
I B M O E E M N A V Y P P O P E C T I E C
R D A R T A F L I A Y R R E H C N I S K K
E E L S T L T O G A H T A E N I S E H O O
C C F O D P E P P E R B U R G U N D Y A P
```

BEETROOT	FIRE ENGINE	MAROON	RUBY
BEGONIA	FLAME	MEAT	TITIAN
BLUSH	FUCHSIA	MULBERRY	TOMATO
BURGUNDY	GARNET	PEPPER	VERMILION
CERISE	HENNA	PLUM	WINE
CHERRY	KETCHUP	POPPY	
CLARET	LADYBIRD	POSTBOX	
CORAL	LIPSTICK	RADISH	
CRANBERRY	LOBSTER	RHUBARB	
CRIMSON	MAGENTA	ROUGE	

26
Winter Worries

Can you find all the listed winter words in the grid? When you've found them all, write out the leftover letters from top to bottom in the spaces below the grid in order to spell the punchline to the joke.

```
C A F N L L I H C D N I W E A T H E R F F
S K R H F R E E Z E P I P T S R U B R F T
E N O O Y O S N O W B O A R D U S O 1 H S
O I Z W E K A L F W O N S R G U S T A E O
H R E L S N O W M O B I L E G T S I I A R
S G N I N R O M Y T S O R F E N L C N V F
W N P N C O L D F R O N T D E S I A M Y A
O I I G T H I C K S N O W Z T N G R E S M
N T P W Y K S Y A R G I O O E G L L U N R
S A E I Y R R U L F N R N S O I G L O O E
C K G N I I K S F D F E S B R E T N I W P
A S R D N A M W O N S L O N G N I G H T S
D E E P S N O W G N I T A K S E C I R O T
```

BURST PIPE	FROZEN STIFF	LONG NIGHTS	SNOWSHOES
COLD FRONT	GRAY SKY	PERMAFROST	THICK SNOW
DEEP SNOW	GUST	POURING RAIN	TOBOGGAN
FLURRY	HAILSTONES	SKATING RINK	WEATHER
FOG	HEAVY SNOW	SKIING	WIND CHILL
FREEZE	HOWLING WIND	SNOWBOARD	WINTER
FROSTED WINDOW	ICE-SKATING	SNOWFLAKE	
FROSTY MORNINGS	ICINESS	SNOWMAN	
FROZEN PIPE	IGLOO	SNOWMOBILE	

What did one snowman say to the other snowman?

____ ___ _____ _____?

27
Snack Time

Looking for tasty sandwich fillings? We've got loads of delicious and unique sandwich fillings. See if you can find all the ingredients below.

ANCHOVY
AVOCADO
BACON
BEEF
BLT
BRIE
CHEESE
CHICKEN
CHUTNEY
CIABATTA
COLESLAW
CRAB
CUCUMBER
EGG MAYO
FRIED EGG
JELLY
LETTUCE
MOZZARELLA
MUSTARD
ONION
PANINI
PASTRAMI
PEANUT BUTTER
PEPPER
PICKLE
RELISH

SALAMI	SAUSAGE	STEAK	TUNA
SALMON	SHRIMP	SWISS	TURKEY
SARDINE	SPREAD	TOMATO	

```
D J E O F D W N S A L A M I D E N
R A S O Y G F O T A M O T D L I N
R H E I C A O V O N L R I K S N O
D L E R B H M R G D N M C I Y I S
P H H A P T I G E O A I O M L N T
R A C N U S Y C G E P C O N L A U
R O S R L E S W K E O Z O E E P N
N E K T N T S R S E Z Y F V J N A
E E P T R A S W H A N V S L A L A
Y O U P R A A G R H T O T R E E T
N H I D E L M E I Y S H E E O T T
C D I L S P L I M R T C A N I T A
E N S E O L R E P T H N K L F U B
E U L I A R E L I S H A G N R C A
A O R E T T U B T U N A E P I E I
C N O I N O E S C U C U M B E R C
B S A U S A G E W D S K V O D R T
L E I A E N I F L I B A R C E S R
T E E O A R D R A T S U M W G T I
H N Y F B U E D L S R S G A G M O
```

A Day at the Zoo

Have a go at finding all of these zoo-related words in the grid.

```
L Q B S S L G T P O H S T F I G D S S T R B
E C T G D I S I U O N S A N T A K R E E M S
M S O O Y N W G R O O A O N I H R K P C R A
A A R H D C O N O A Y Z L N D S C T H O R Q
C R T T S O H I M R F A D U E I I A T T E U
H B O R E L S U A E I F D L T L E A F T P A
I E I A L N N G C U N L E Y E N G G E E E R
M Z S W G P O N A B E P L H L I A S O R E I
P W E E A A I E W M H I O A L C F R D Z K U
A R N N E R L P U A M U E L S L H K A U O M
N R D G D K A R N A S E A V I A R Y O T O O
Z A A N L Z E T F E C A P T I V I T Y O Z S
E C Y E A O S N O I T A V R E S N O C C R D
E L R T B O N F E E D I N G T I M E I E B B
```

ALLIGATORS
AQUARIUM
AVIARY
BALD EAGLES
BROOKFIELD ZOO
CAFE
CAGE
CAMEL
CAPTIVITY
CHIMPANZEE
CONSERVATION
DAY OUT

ELEPHANT
FAMILY TICKET
FEEDING TIME
GIFT SHOP
GIRAFFE
GORILLA
LEMUR
LINCOLN PARK ZOO
MACAW
MEERKAT
OTTER
PANDA

PENGUIN
REPTILE HOUSE
RHINO
SAN DIEGO ZOO
SEA LION SHOWS
TARANTULA
TORTOISE
WARTHOGS
ZEBRA
ZOOKEEPER

29
Feeling Thirsty?

One of these drinks can be found three times in the grid – which one?

```
Q L E G H V S L E C I U J T I U R F
P E D S E C I C O C A C O L A E L E
O M A E T G N T B R A E R L T G I C
P O Y D I S A U A P A O T A W H M I
T N R A R H N T P M O N W D C Y E U
O A R E P L T L O T I C G N E K J J
M D E M S E E O B R I N E E O C U E
A E H I I J P E O N A U W C A S I G
T N C L U S E S O M Q D R A S D C N
O L G I B R P T I N S H E F T S E A
J V C R A N B E R R Y J U I C E L R
U E P E P S I N P P E R R I E R R O
I K N I R D Y Z Z I F T E B R E H S
C S D I A L O O K T P U N E V E S Y
E M I L K S H A K E D L F A N T A G
```

APPLE JUICE	FRUIT PUNCH	ORANGE JUICE	SHERBET
CHERRYADE	GATORADE	ORANGEADE	SMOOTHIE
COCA-COLA	ICED TEA	PEPSI	SPRITE
COKE	KOOL-AID	PERRIER	TOMATO JUICE
CRANBERRY JUICE	LEMONADE	POP	TONIC WATER
FANTA	LIME JUICE	QUENCH	VITAMIN WATER
FIZZY DRINK	LIMEADE	ROOT BEER	
FRUIT JUICE	MILK-SHAKE	SEVEN UP	

The drink that can be found three times is _____!

Happy Halloween

Can you find all the listed Halloween costumes? When you've found them all, write out the leftover letters from top to bottom in the spaces below the grid in order to spell the joke and its punchline.

```
Y W E S C A R E C R O W E Y M M U M F D H
E L T R N A M O W D L O N T P E D O R R G
S E I S N A G N P F H U G R A A N E A A E
K T H M O I E O A M A M I H A R V I N Z N
E G W L A E K I B H H S I T O I I D K I I
L N W V U F R P C L O P A S L S R P E W E
E I O Q A Y S E M N I C R J L A T E N N Z
T K N H L M R M E U K N E I G F L E S I O
O T S I C P P R A C P S T O N E R B T D M
N S V A E T T I A D T T N H E C A G E D B
H E O L S T I L R E D M O N S T E R I A I
D O G R E O B W R E F A L E G N A S N L E
F I F L O W E R E W C M E R M A I D S A E
```

ADDAMS FAMILY	FAIRY	MUMMY	SCARECROW
ALADDIN	FRANKENSTEIN	OGRE	SNOW WHITE
ANGEL	GENIE	OLD WOMAN	VAMPIRE
BAT	GHOST	PRINCESS	WEREWOLF
BLACK CAT	GOBLIN	PIRATE	WITCH
DEVIL	KING	PRISONER	WIZARD
DRAGON	LEPRECHAUN	PUMPKIN	ZOMBIE
ELF	MERMAID	QUEEN	
EVIL JESTER	MONSTER	SKELETON	

_ _ _ _ _ _ _ _ _ _ _ _ _ _ _ _ _ _

_ _ _ _ _ _ _ _ _ _ _ _ _ _ _ ?

_ _ _ _ _ _ _ _ _ _ _ _ _ _ _ _ !

Blue

See if you can find all of these things that are
connected to the color blue in the grid.

```
D P G A L F H S I T T O C S E R I B B O N
N E O C E A N L A G O O N D M I Y D A R T
O R G M A A M C D R R B U T S I V P I H C
O I T V E S A U R I O E E N J M O O B A A
M W T J L Y A C I T D N E R A G U L M D M
N I E V L N C P T N N I L K Y I U R N S C
A N O U E O H L P O I H T R F E T A F A O
I K S W W T E E B H A H O C B L R N P S L
D L A A D L E T S R I R P E F A A A E N L
I E T S E I S O E N G R R L C H B G T G A
S E M K E T E B H T I R E A E W U E E A R
R S N R P S E N I Y Y R J S E D O C R D A
R U K T S L N S U E D E S H O E S I E E A
F S O Y L R N I P U L E G N I K C O T S T
```

BERET	GENTIAN	MOVIE	SKY
BLUEBERRY	GREEK FLAG	OCEAN	SMURFS
BONNET	HAREBELL	PERIWINKLE	SPEEDWELL
BOTTLE	JACARANDA	PETER	STILTON
CHEESE	JAY	RIBBON	STOCKING
CHIP	JEANS	RINSE	SUEDE SHOES
COLLAR	LAGOON	SAPPHIRE	VEIN
DELPHINIUM	LUPIN	SCOTTISH FLAG	WATER
FUNK	MOON	SEA	WHALE

32
Picnic Puzzle

Can you find all the listed picnic words in the grid below? When you've found them all, write out the leftover letters from top to bottom in the spaces below the grid to spell the joke and its punchline.

```
B L A N K E T W F H Y D U M B R E L L A
I R I A H S E R F O N A P K I N R D O B
T E K S A B R E W O L F D L I W E T C A
H E E D I S T U O E T D Y O E H L D S C
M V E G E T A R I A N L I X A T B E E K
T Y B H O T B L S R F U C N K O M C R P
W E R C S K R O C R E U L C G L U K F A
R N E E S D M E E H R P A B I C T C L C
E O E T L R N T S S S P M E A E H H A K
L T Z W E T T U I S E T B A H L E A S A
O R E H L U U O O C E A A K H B D I I D
O A T R B E N C I R S D K E S A I R N R
C C O N T A I N E R G G E R E T T A L P
```

AL FRESCO	CLAMBAKE	FOLDING CHAIR	TABLECLOTH
BACKPACK	CONTAINER	FRESH AIR	THERMOS
BASKET	COOLER	GROUNDSHEET	TUMBLER
BEAKER	CORKSCREW	HAMPER	UMBRELLA
BLANKET	CUTLERY	ICE PACK	VEGETARIAN
BREEZE	DECK CHAIR	NAPKIN	WILD FLOWER
BUTTERFLY	DESSERT	OUTSIDE	
CARTON	EXCURSION	PLATTER	

___ ___ ___ _____ _____?

__ ___ __ _____ _____!

Fruit...

See if you can find all these fruits in the top grid.

BANANA
CHERRY
KIWI
LIME
MANDARIN
MANGO
MELON
NECTARINE
PEACH

PEAR
PINEAPPLE
PLUM
PRUNE
RASPBERRY
SATSUMA
STRAWBERRY
TANGERINE

```
Y R R E B W A R T S D
K O S O P L U M A D L
S P O R T H I T L G S
O I U Y T C S M D S O
L N B T R U H U E Y I
E E S A M R O T R E E
N A T A N G E R I N E
I P C D L A E H G I I
R P E S O B N T C R K
A L I O P E H A L A I
D E H S G C U N S T W
N E A O A N C D T C I
A R P E A R A I B E E
M L P N O L E M G N N
```

34

...and Nut

Now see if you can find all of these nuts in the lower grid.

ACORN
ALMOND
BEECHNUT
BUTTERNUT
CASHEW
CHESTNUT
COBNUT
COCONUT
COLA NUT

FILBERT
GROUNDNUT
HAZELNUT
MACADAMIA
PEANUT
PECAN
PINE NUT
PISTACHIO
WALNUT

```
C D N O M L A G F Z S
T A M A C A D A M I A
N U S T U N L A W T R
S R N H E R N I G U E
B T O H E A G C R N S
C U E C C W H D O L T
O N T E A E T P U E U
C B P T S R E R N Z N
O O I T E A S B D A A
N C N B N R E L N H L
U U L U R I N Z U E O
T I T S E D L U T R C
F G P I N E N U T M I
O I H C A T S I P E S
```

35
Barbecue

Can you find the listed barbecue words in the grid?

```
Y Q O U T S I D E T C S I Z Z L E Y B E R
R L P U T H G I L C H R E M M U S R T T
B E A R I A H C D E A D R I N K I T D A
S E T O T A E H D S R E B M E C E N Y L
N P C H C O O K I N G O I L K U A A K P
E A A A G R S N R I R S P B Q B D I O W
D M P T R I A K G W I N U I S I T R C E
R Y A K U E L H E S L I R U L C T A S L
A O N L I L F E C W L B H O H A S T E L
G S O M F N A U R T E N H E B S M E R D
B A R B E C U E L I D R N L O P O G F O
N O I T A T I V N I F B E A C H K E L N
G R E A S E V N R O B H G I E N E V A E
```

AL FRESCO	FIRE LIGHTER	NAPKIN	SKEWER
BARBECUE	FLAME	NEIGHBOR	SMOKE
BE CAREFUL	GARDEN	OUTSIDE	SPATULA
BEACH	GREASE	PLATE	SUMMER
BRICK BUILT	GRIDDLE	PORTABLE	VEGETARIAN
BRIQUETTE	HEAT	SIZZLE	WELL DONE
CHAIR	HOLIDAY		
CHARCOAL	HUSBAND		
CHARGRILLED	INSECT		
COOKING OIL	INVITATION		
DRINK	KITCHEN		
EMBERS	LIGHT UP		

36
We All Scream For...

All these words are flavors of ICE CREAM.

APPLE
BANANA
BLUEBERRY
BUBBLEGUM
CAPPUCCINO
CARAMEL
CHEESECAKE
CHOCOLATE
COCONUT
COFFEE
ELDERBERRY
FOREST FRUIT
GOOSEBERRY
HAZELNUT
HONEYCOMB
LEMON
LICORICE
LIME
MANGO
MAPLE NUT
MARSHMALLOW
MINT
ORANGE
PEANUT
PISTACHIO
PRALINE
RASPBERRY

RHUBARB
RUM FUDGE
TIRAMISU
TOBLERONE
TOFFEE
TUTTI FRUTTI
VANILLA

K	R	U	M	F	U	D	G	E	G	N	A	R	O	W	V
L	A	A	T	M	C	A	P	P	U	C	C	I	N	O	Z
I	N	D	L	I	A	O	I	H	C	A	T	S	I	P	D
C	A	S	E	L	U	R	U	S	I	M	A	R	I	T	D
O	N	C	T	E	I	R	S	S	A	P	P	L	E	T	B
R	A	H	A	M	T	N	F	H	S	D	S	P	T	U	R
I	B	E	L	O	T	T	A	T	M	K	R	U	B	N	A
C	T	E	O	N	U	O	O	V	S	A	N	B	Y	O	S
E	U	S	C	W	R	F	O	B	L	E	L	R	B	C	P
R	N	E	O	D	F	F	G	I	L	E	R	L	S	O	B
H	L	C	H	S	I	E	N	P	G	E	U	O	O	C	E
U	E	A	C	I	T	E	A	U	B	E	R	E	F	W	R
B	Z	K	G	U	T	M	M	R	B	D	S	O	M	I	R
A	A	E	N	M	U	V	E	E	F	F	O	C	N	I	Y
R	H	A	I	N	T	D	R	I	C	A	R	A	M	E	L
B	E	N	S	Y	L	R	H	O	N	E	Y	C	O	M	B
P	T	D	L	E	Y	R	R	E	B	E	S	O	O	G	G

Pooch Puzzle

All but one of the different dog breeds can be found in the grid. Can you find the missing one?

ALSATIAN	BULLDOG	DINGO	POINTER	SHEEPDOG
BASSET	CHIHUAHUA	DOBERMAN	POM	SPANIEL
BEAGLE	CHOW	GREYHOUND	POODLE	SPRINGER
BOXER	COLLIE	HUSKY	PUG	TERRIER
	CORGI	LABRADOR	SALUKI	WHIPPET
	DALMATIAN	MASTIFF	SETTER	
		MONGREL		

```
          C E R                                    K D B
        Y F H E M                                N A G U D
    M A S T I F F                              S L R O L I R
    K O P O R H U                              M S E D L N H
    W P P I R T U S C D H R L I M Z A A P T P D G T
      D O B E R M A N E L D O O P T O L A N E O O
      X S T O C U H U S K Y D I U G S N I E G
      S J N O O I K U L A S A A W G A I O H S
      A J G L H D R V D A B N Q W R H T E P S R H
    B V R L Y R E G N I R P S L Z W B I L B O X E R
    A E I E K T W                              A P C O R G I
    L E R N T O X                              N L P P V T J
    G Y E H C                                  A Q E E U
    S C B                                      F G T
```

The missing dog breed is _____ !

38
Islands

Find all the island-related words in the grid, but watch out, because there is a very popular island in Florida hiding in the grid that isn't in the list.

BEACH
CASTAWAY
CAVE
COASTLINE
COCONUT
CORAL
COVE
CRAB
DESERTED
DIVING
DOLPHIN
DRIFTWOOD
FISH
FRUIT
HUT
IDYLLIC
JETTY
LAGOON
PALM TREE
PARADISE
PEACEFUL

```
J G B M C L U F E C A E P E W B
G M P E P I S H E L T E R N A N
B G N A A M L N Y W N O D R T T
D S G S L C M L H J H B O N E U
L N E R S M H I Y S E C O I R N
A A A T U R T L E D A T W T F O
C N R L I E G R E V I S T O A C
I T C Y S N R L E D G N F Y L O
P M I A I I I S E E D A I O L C
O U N V S O O S T E R S R P N L
R D I E P T E C D E H A D A B A
T D B S D R A U R E I S O R E G
F H N A T A L W L A R O C A F O
R U U E R C H L A T M R A D E O
U N D T E C I S E Y S O G I E N
I F I S H M N I H P L O D S R T
T E V O C O A S T L I N E E U A
```

REEF   SHADE   SHORE   UNSPOILED
SEA   SHELL   TROPICAL   WATERFALL
SECLUDED   SHELTER   TURTLE   WHITE SAND

The popular island in Florida that you can find in the grid is

_____ _____!

39
Shipshape

Can you find the listed types of boat in the grid? When you've found them all, write out the leftover letters from top to bottom in the spaces below the grid to spell the answer to the joke at the bottom of the page.

```
N W O T J H R I D D P D T N H C T E K H
P G A U D E E E I I I A H C I R T T J Y
I I N T K R S T H N O N A O R U R P R D
H K H N E T E S T B I T G E W I C I E R
S C A S R R E A E E A T G H M S O H K O
P T N O G L T S D M V D N A Y E A S A F
O U Y U T N U A A N E R R A O S S G E O
O E S T A O O R X R O A O N G H T A R I
R T A W H L A L D I N U A C U I E L B L
T B A N A N A B O A T C G A T P R F E V
T A O B G N I H S I F E T H C A Y B C D
J E T F O I L P I H S L L A T R E N I L
K A Y A K C A R G O S H I P I H S R A W
```

BANANA BOAT	DESTROYER	ICEBREAKER	TANKER
BATTLESHIP	DHOW	JETFOIL	TRIMARAN
BRIGANTINE	DINGHY	JUNK	TROOPSHIP
CANOE	DREADNOUGHT	KAYAK	TUG
CARGO SHIP	DREDGER	KETCH	WARSHIP
CATAMARAN	FISHING BOAT	LAUNCH	WATER TAXI
COASTER	FLAGSHIP	LINER	YACHT
CORVETTE	HOUSEBOAT	LONGSHIP	
CRUISE SHIP	HYDROFOIL	TALL SHIP	

What did the sea say to the sailing ship?

_ _ _ _ _ _ _ _ , _ _ _ _ _ _ _ _ _ _ _ _ !

40

Come...

All of these words start with the letters COM.

COMBS	COMPACT
COMBUST	COMPANY
COMEDY	COMPASS
COMELY	COMPETE
COMET	COMPEL
COMFY	COMPLY
COMIC	COMPORT
COMING	COMPOSE
COMMA	COMPOST
COMMEND	COMPRESS
COMMIT	COMPUTE
COMMON	COMRADE

```
G F C C O M P A N Y C R Y
I R C O M E L Y I O T E F
T S O P M O C A M L S C M
R I E N A M U P R O U O O
C C I D A S A L P G B M C
T O N D A S S M R A M P O
C M M I S R O E N T O L M
A M Y P E C M C R C C Y P
P E D C U S O O O P L A E
M N E O B T P M C M M B L
O D M M R M E U M I M O E
C N O I O T S G N I M O C
A C C C O M P E T E T E N
```

41

```
E G C E G U O G M F Y V S
N O A L O D N O G S L C S
O O T I G O U L A S H O N
G D M E E O N G G T A O G
G S G R M R D O O C R O G
C O O N E R L L H A D I O
I G B V I D U T Y F L A G
H N O B G O A O A G S L G
T G E O L I G T G O T L L
O A R R L E H U I B E I E
G S N O S E A T Y L E R C
E R G M R G O A D E I O N
E A G O B L I N S T T G R
```

...and Go

And all of these words begin with the letters GO.

GOAD	GOLIATH
GOAL	GONE
GOAT	GONDOLA
GOBBLE	GOOD
GOBLET	GORE
GOBLIN	GORILLA
GODFATHER	GORSE
GODLY	GOTHIC
GOGGLE	GOUGE
GOING	GOULASH
GOLD	GOURMET
GOLF	GOVERN

42
Treasure Map

Look for all the places in the pirate treasure map. When you've found them all, write down the leftover letters to spell out the name of a famous pirate.

ABYSS
BLUFF
CANAL
CHASM
CLIFF
COPSE
DALE
DELTA
DOWN
DUMP
DUNE
FEN
GLADE
GORGE
HILL
MARSH
MESA
MOUND
MOUNTAIN
NORTH
PATH
RIDGE
RIVER
SEABED

SLOPE
SOUTH

STREAM
SWAMP

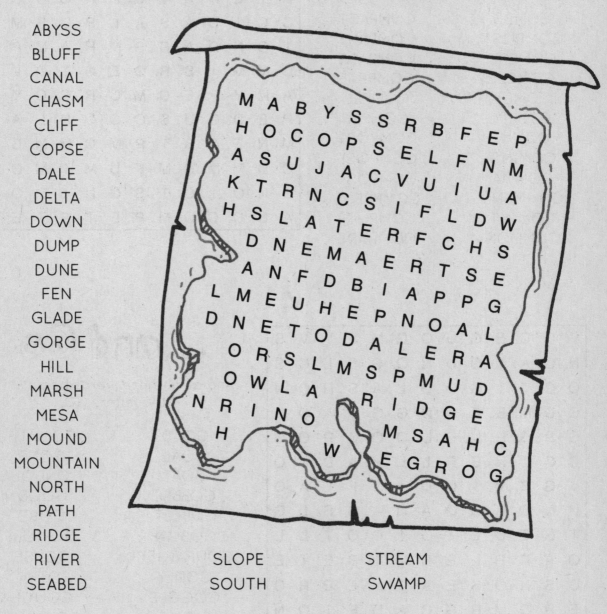

The friendly pirate is _____ _____!

43
Jewel

Now that this pirate has found his hidden treasure, can you help him find all the jewel-related words in the grid? Once you've finished, the leftover letters will spell out a joke and its punchline!

AMULET
BANGLE
BRACELET

BROOCH
CAMEO
CHOKER
CROWN
CRYSTAL

DIAMANTE
DIAMOND
EMERALD
JEWEL
LOCKET
NECKLACE
PEARL
RING
RUBY
SAPPHIRE
TIARA

```
                G E
              E D N T
            L I W H I N
          G A A L T T R A
        N M I S R I T E J M
      A O E B R A C E L E T A
    B N V E C R E N L H W H A I
  R D D E R A K P T U H E C A N D
  L A T S Y R C L S M A L O D L I
  O N W O R C A A A M O O A N
  C H O K E R P C D P R Y
  K A Y I C P N E E B
    E G F A H O M U
      T R M I E R
        I E R T
          O E
```

_____ _ , _____ _____ _____ _____

_ _____ ?

_____ ___ __ !

44
Harry Potter Puzzle

Test your Harry Potter know-how by finding all the words in the Hogwart's Express. When you've found them all, try and match the words with their definitions below.

1 Screaming plant that helps return people who have been transfigured into the shape they were before.

2 Malfoy's house elf.

3 Group of Dark wizards who are followers of Voldemort.

4 Wizard prison.

5 Position on Quidditch team. They keep Bludgers away.

6 Society for the Promotion of Elfish Welfare.

7 Key position on a Quidditch team. This player must catch the Golden Snitch.

8 Screaming, scolding letter sent by an owl.

9 Where wizards and witches shop for supplies.

10 Quidditch position. Players try to score with the Quaffle.

11 A witch or wizard who can change into an animal.

12 Giant spider living in the Forbidden Forest.

13 Professor Dumbledore's phoenix.

14 Non-magical person.

15 Coins; a form of wizard money.

16 Wizards' bank.

17 Quidditch goal-scoring ball.

18 Quidditch ball that's fast and hard to catch.

19 Three-headed dog guarding the Philosopher's Stone.

20 State-of-the-art racing broom that can go faster than the Nimbus 2000.

21 A monstrous serpent.

22 Dark wizard catcher.

23 Ordinary Wizarding Levels. Exams taken at 15.

24 Dark, cloaked, faceless creatures from Azkaban. Their kiss will suck a person's soul.

25 Beautiful female creatures that can enchant men and boys.

26 Wife of Aragog.

27 Hagrid's pet boarhound.

28 Shape-shifting monster; takes the form of whatever it thinks will frighten those near it.

29 Quidditch player who guards the posts.

30 Someone who has no magical powers even though born into a magical family.

31 Witch or wizard who can talk to and understand snakes.

32 Quidditch ball that tries to knock players off their broomsticks.

33 Gigantic snake whose venom is used by Voldemort as food.

Word Search Grid

```
                        M P E N D S C J H Q S
                        A C Y I X Z L T D N X
                        Z Z A J I I U W O P G
    P L W         B D   S G K N A O Y E O L X
    M C E               O T I A M F L U F F Y
    Q O P               H G T L B L N
V L W S H F R B E N H G T L B L N
A N I M A G U S A M A O E O A A S
B I E B R D K L K N E S W G G E N
K Q L L V E L D E W R N U L K N C
K O G U T E T E E A K U T W E S I O T R D
S F G D Y S R A P B S L A O H R X R P S O
G B U G E R Z T E A I F F D R S V W G W B
O X M E K Q K H R B L E E P K S S E F J B
V G K R A V Z E W M I T L O B E R I F O Y
G E N L R E S A H C S H C T I N S A G Y C
R A E Y D H G T Q U A F F L E T U G O M
T S L N D M E A U B N H V G R A T G I
Y Q O A I Z R           H O R G N A F
N R O M E F S           R T A I A R D
    S Q U I B           U U J J A
```

ANIMAGUS   DIAGON ALLEY   MOSAG

ARAGOG   DOBBY   MUGGLE

AUROR   FANG   NAGINI

AZKABAN   FAWKES   OWLS

BASILISK   FIREBOLT   PARSELMOUTH

BEATER   FLUFFY   QUAFFLE

BLUDGER   GALLEONS   SEEKER

BOGGART   GRINGOTTS   SNITCH

CHASER   HOWLER   SPEW

DEATH EATERS   KEEPER   SQUIB

DEMENTORS   MANDRAKE   VEELA

45
Motel

It's summer so it's time to go to your favorite resort. Relax and take it easy with this motel-themed puzzle.

ALARM CALL
ALL-INCLUSIVE
BREAKFAST
DINNER
ELEVATOR
FULL BOARD
GARDEN
GOLF COURSE
GYMNASIUM
JACUZZI
KEY
KIDS CLUB
LOUNGE
LUNCH
MONEY CHANGING
PARASOL
PARKING
PETS WELCOME
RESTAURANT
ROOM SERVICE
SAUNA
SEA VIEW
SNACK BAR
SPA
SWIMMING POOL
TERRACE
VACANCY

```
J H T H S T D L W G N I K R A P
G P T H D W O E T T I R P H D E
I N T E E U I O I T O K F B B T
E D I R N V H M I O O T E E U S
P R E G A L A R M C A L L Y L W
F I E E N H V S S I O T T Y C E
U E S E C A E A S D N R N M S L
L I L N T R H N C A S G H E D C
L A U E V S A C R A R S P A I O
B L N I V C A U Y E N O T O K M
O R C U K A A F N E N C E M O E
A E B B A T T N K I N P Y U J L
R S A W S S I O O A E O D I A E
D R T E R D G A R D E N M S C C
E S R U O C F L O G F R N A U A
I E S O G M H T R E N I B N Z R
A L L I N C L U S I V E Y M Z R
S E O D R T P N I E B S O Y I E
R E T H L I L O S A R A P G G T
```

46
Table Tennis

Try to find all the words listed below in the grid.

```
E M A G Y Y D H F D E E K O R T S R A S
W R R H N B Y I D P R A C T I C E L T M
L O S E A O A T K N U A S L P F G O P A
F T K A T T P C M A T C H E E I H D U S
S I N C O U I G K H S U O R L S R Y M H
I T B S A L R A N S O P E L P B L G R S
D E S O F T N N T I P E E O B L U I A I
E P B A U U T S Y O P I R E A A E O W N
S M D L M N E A N L R D N R G S L N D G
P O I P O T C E A D N A H K C A B L R L
I C I H N C N E E O E R O C S U A R I E
N R N O E T K S W E R V E A I L T W V S
E O C G N I M I T E D S E R V I C E E T
```

ATTACK	GAME	SCORE
BACKHAND	GRIP	SERVICE
BACKSPIN	HIT	SIDE SPIN
BALL	LOSE	SINGLES
BLOCK	MATCH	SMASH
BOUNCE	OPPONENT	STROKE
COMPETITOR	PING-PONG	SWERVE
CONTEST	POSTURE	TABLE
DOUBLES	PRACTICE	TIMING
DRIVE	RALLY	TOSS
DROP SHOT	REFEREE	UMPIRE
FLICK	RETURN	WARM-UP

47
Spot the Sports

Can you find the listed sports in the grid? When you've found them all, write out the leftover letters from top to bottom in the spaces below the grid to spell out a joke and its punchline.

```
B O W L I N G T V O L L E Y B A L L B H
B L L O L L A B E G D O D A W L D I L L
A L O L O L B A C T S R S S L E L B L A
D A L A A L A R L E H K U A P L H L A C
M B O B L B I B L G E E B G I A A Y B R
I T P E A C T B T T N E R A B B N T E O
N F R S K S R E B O L O R B K Y D E L S
T O E E I A E A U F O D P C A R B U D S
O S T S M N L B F Q S F I G S L A Q D E
N T A A Y L N I A C C T O O N L L O A B
Y S W I T T W E I L S A N G B I L R P Y
T S C I T E L H T A L H R E F A P C N S
```

ATHLETICS   CRICKET   MARBLES   STICKBALL
BADMINTON   CROQUET   PADDLE BALL   TENNIS
BASEBALL   DODGEBALL   PING-PONG   TETHERBALL
BASKETBALL   FOOTBALL   RACQUET BALL   VOLLEYBALL
BILLIARDS   HANDBALL   RUGBY   WATER POLO
BOWLING   LACROSSE   SOFTBALL   WIFFLE BALL

___ ___ _____

_____ ____ _____?

__ _____ __ ___ _____!

Baked...

Can you find all of these things that can be baked in the top grid?

BAGEL
BAGUETTE
BRIOCHE
BRUSCHETTA
BUN
CAKE
CHAPATI
CINNAMON ROLL
CORNBREAD
CROISSANT
CRUMPET

FLATBREAD
FOCACCIA
MUFFIN
PANINI
PARATHA
PIE
PITA
PIZZA
SCONE
TEA BREAD

```
K P S F L B B D E G S
D I S L L R O A T I P
A Z L A L I E E G N P
H Z S T O O N R U E O
T A C B R C O B E D L
A C D R N H C A A L F
R H G E O E S E M O B
A A H A M I R T C I A
P P N D A B S A E S G
P A N I N I C S O R U
I T E R N C E K A C E
L I O N I F F U M N T
N C S A C R U M P E T
B R U S C H E T T A E
```

...Beans

See if you can find all of these types of bean in the bottom grid.

BAKED
BROAD
BUTTER
COCOA
COFFEE
FRENCH
GREEN
HARICOT
JELLY

JUMPING
KIDNEY
LIMA
MUNG
OLD
PINTO
RUNNER
SOY
STRING

```
S R E T T U B S A A S
H J I A S L S T M D D
P E A O I S E I L L A
T L Y A H I L E S O O
O L J U M P I N G H R
A Y D E K A B T A E B
D L Y R M E I R N E A
P S O E E T I M U N G
F R I F N C E L R G H
C R F N O D U A U N P
N O E T E S I E N I O
C C C N D E R K N R T
I A B O C E R T E T L
G N M S A H O G R S K
```

50
Games

All the games listed below can be found twice in the grid.

```
F W J Z U I S E E H C R A P L N P O K E R
L T U T G S L N T F I E L U A C N E D R T
I E L N S G R T B I E P W M N H Y U E D L
R A I E T E N N A A R S G E I E C I D L T
F A H B E C D O N R C N H S U C I T E P A
L C A N A S T A J N A K R E I K S O A T Y
E C D L R G O N I H S A G K H E E O U T R
N E A B I L L P S W A O E A C R D T R F A
N I E S D Y L O G H T M P U M S A R E N I
Y S E M O A C D A L R A T P N M I E A B E
S O A R S H E G T H R U L R I G O N M O G
A I E Y O T C D O T S S K O E R T N I N D
D A E L R Z N F E F C L S R E T O P A U I
W T I O R E H S N R I Y U E C D S L S R R
G A M P Y E U O A B E S I J T N A I R E B
S O L O I O T B N E C D H A H R U P W S E
O I L N M A B T G N S E O N I M O D M T E
R F S O K L O I Y S O L I T A I R E A B E
C D N M E T L R H E S U A I O N T E P R W
```

BACKGAMMON	DOMINOES	OLD MAID	TWISTER
BRIDGE	GO FISH	PARCHEESI	UNO
CANASTA	HANGMAN	POKER	YAHTZEE
CHECKERS	MAH-JONGG	SCRABBLE	
CHESS	MONOPOLY	SOLITAIRE	
DICE	MOUSE TRAP	SORRY	

51
Farm

One of the listed words appears three times in the grid. Which one is it?

ARABLE
BALE
BARN
BREED
CATTLE
CEREAL
CORNFIELD
CROP
DRAINAGE
FALLOW
FARMLAND
FERTILIZER
FLOCK
FODDER
FOWL
FURROW
GRAZE
HARVEST
HAYSTACK
HERD
LIVESTOCK
PASTURE
PIGSTY
PLOW
POULTRY
REAP

SCARECROW
SHEEP
SILAGE

SOIL
STILE
STRAW

THRESH
TRACTOR
VEGETABLE

WHEAT

```
Y M C E R E A L N N N M N U L W
R R S P O R C N T H R E S H W O
T M E I I N R I U N I N M I O L
L E N Z L W O R C E R A C S F P
U F L Y I A P U I N S I G M G D
O O N B S L G H U R O T C A R T
P D I N A P I E A E I W H E A T
D D S O E R F T L R H Y D G Z N
N E M E I U A B R A V S A K E K
A R H L R H A O Y E U E N E C A
L S B R I T I S S O F E S O C D
M T O A E V T E N I E S L T O O
R W G G M A E H R T U F P O R C
A A E E C N W S I U E B A R N S
F V Y K E O O D T L T A T N F P
H E I E A S L D T O B S O E I S
T E L I T S L T E R C L A G E T
H D R A I N A G E E I K S P L R
U I G D B C F A N O R T M A D A
E C D S K V P O S T Y B I A E W
```

The word that appears three times is _____!

Check It Out

Can you find the listed words that begin with CH (like chocolate) in the grid?
When you've found them all, the leftover letters from top to bottom will spell out
the punchline to the joke under the grid.

```
P C C C H A C H E S T S H E E S A H C W
A N H H C C N D R A O B S S E H C E A R
H I A A A H N I C C E C H A R A C T E R
C A M O L N I I H H S R C F L I R E C E
H H P S A I D E F C A H O E O I H H L C
I C I R C H C E F F A N N H A C I C H C
L E O C I K S E L L A N C H C M I E E H
D K N H M O E I L I A H C E N N R V G A
C C M O E L H E R H E I C E O U I N R M
H U U O H G N C C E C R Y R B H R U A B
E H H S C G M K L A H C H I C K E N H E
F C C E E Y E N T U H C B Y T N A H C R
```

CHAFFINCH	CHANCE	CHASE	CHEST	CHOIR
CHAIN	CHANDELIER	CHEER	CHICKEN	CHOOSE
CHAIR	CHANNEL	CHEF	CHIEF	CHORE
CHALICE	CHANT	CHEMICAL	CHILD	CHRONICLE
CHALK	CHAOS	CHECK	CHIMNEY	CHUCK
CHALLENGE	CHAP	CHERISH	CHINA	CHUM
CHAMBER	CHARACTER	CHERUB	CHIVE	CHUTNEY
CHAMPION	CHARGE	CHESSBOARD	CHOICE	

Why did the chocolate chip cookie go to the doctor?

___ ___ _____ _____!

53
NBA

The NBA Finals is the championship series of the National Basketball Association. The series is played between the winners of the Western and Eastern Conference Finals. See if you can find all the names from both Conferences.

WEST

BLAZERS
CLIPPERS
GRIZZLIES
JAZZ
KINGS
MAVERICKS
LAKERS
NUGGETS
PELICANS
ROCKETS
SPURS
SUNS
TIMBERWOLVES
THUNDER
WARRIORS

EAST

BOBCATS
BUCKS
BULLS
CAVALIERS
CELTICS
HAWKS
HEAT
KNICKS
MAGIC
NETS
PACERS
PISTONS
RAPTORS
SEVENTY-
SIXERS
WIZARDS

```
Y J X P E L I C A N S
D G M N B O D O C S L
H O R U U K Y A D R L
S S C I N G V M S E U
P K K I Z A G R N K B
S I C W L Z O E O A S
H K S I A I L N T L E
S O E T R H D I N S V
M R O R O E T S E E E
S H A N S N V T Y S N
J W S T E N S A E D T
A A S O V I P C M T Y
E T Z R L N U B A E S
O H S Z O I R O L R I
T U G D W T S B E R X
S N U S R R P C M O E
A D E D E A A A N C R
H E U Z B P Z I R K S
O R A T M A G I C E T
E L A K I N G S W T A
B C E L T I C S L S E
N S R E P P I L C E H
```

Disney Heroines

All the listed heroic female characters below are from Walt Disney productions.
See how quickly you can find them all.

ALICE	DUCHESS	KIARA	PENNY
ANITA	EILONWY	LILO	PERDITA
ANNA	ELSA	MAID MARIAN	POCAHONTAS
ARIEL	ESMERALDA	MEGARA	RAPUNZEL
AURORA	EVE	MELODY	SNOW WHITE
BIANCA	GISELLE	MERIDA	TIANA
CHARLOTTE	HELGA	MINNIE MOUSE	TIGER LILY
CINDERELLA	JANE PORTER	MULAN	TINKER BELL
DAISY DUCK	JASMINE	NALA	VIOLET
DIXIE	JESSIE	NAKOMA	WENDY
DORY	KALA	OLIVIA	

```
Z X H A B N G T B G D U C H E S S H T E Y
C S E R T A I V I O L E T L P E N N Y V R
H G L O M I S W E N D Y E N I M S A J E O
A Y G R E R E B C I K Z K T Y H E E S S D
R W A U G A L S X A N E I C A D S R A L S
L N R A A M L I M U L G R N U S O T I N E
O O A S R D E U P E E L A B I D N L O D A
T L I T A I P A A R R I E E E O Y W E T A
T I K S O A R R L T T A T R H L W S I M O
E E S U O M E I N N I M L A E H L D I L C
N A K O M A L E G A S N C D I D R A I A O
N A L U M Y A L A K L O A T A E N V N L D
E C I L A C N A I B P A E H P O I I I N U
T R B P J A N E P O R T E R S A O L C C A
```

55
Practical Joker

```
W P A C D A M H N
S A N T S A M O I
U N B U F F O O N
C S I Y T E S P C
F R A G N T I V O
O D A R G N E I M
T A E C R U I R P
G E A U K M M N O
E H T D O P E H O
I E E L D O O N P
D L S I L L Y T G
J D D O L C E N D
E D A N L J I O E
S U D O O D N L S
T M W K D K S O O
E N E U E Q U O O
R R P Y E A K F G
```

Some people are always playing practical jokes on others. Can you find all the names that they get called in the grid? If you can, the leftover letters will spell out a joke and its punchline!

BUFFOON	GOOSE	NINNY
CLOD	JESTER	NOODLE
CLOWN	JOKER	NUTTER
CRACKPOT	MADCAP	PUDDING
DONKEY	MUDDLEHEAD	SILLY
DOPE	MUGGINS	TURNIP
FOOL	NINCOMPOOP	

_____ ' _ _ _____ ' _

_____ _____ ?

_____ ____ _____ !

56
Lazy Bones

Hidden in the first grid there are five words that mean LAZY, and in the second grid there are five BONES. How quickly can you find them all?

```
A R N I D L E
O T T C D P Y
S K W R A E S
L Y P E E L S
O R I N A N O
W T A C E R I
I N K S E O T
```

```
E T T D M K F
R E I E R R I
U S T B A A B
M E R D I S U
E E I T A A L
F U E D L R A
S I L L U K S
```

Clumsy or Careful?

Some people think they're very careful, but in fact, they're quite clumsy. Prove to everyone how reliable you are by solving this puzzle.

```
M L U N A B L E G N I L G N U B P S V
X U O M O E F R P S O H I N Y O C S D
M F I T R N A O D P U O C I T S L E C
H E N U N C S R R O D O R I S N E L L
M R S S E E A S K G O O I E A R V E U
D A T F A W G I P R E W L T H H E R M
E C U N K F Y I D Y T T A B U D R A S
L L S W R A E I L O H I F E T A N C Y
I A A R S O N I T G G M A U X B C E D
C N E A T A N R U H E S I O L P T E P
A V A N T R E O I S O N A T Y E E C D
T R G E N M H I R E L I A B L E S R O
E A D K H T L U F L L I K S E T R N T
```

AWKWARD	FORGETFUL	UNABLE
BATTY	GRACEFUL	UNCOORDINATED
BUNGLING	HASTY	
CAREFUL	NEAT	
CARELESS	NEGLIGENT	
CAUTIOUS	RELIABLE	
CLEVER	SAFE	
CLUMSY	SKILLFUL	
DELICATE	SURE	
EXPERT	THOUGHTLESS	

Martial Arts

Can you find all the words related to martial arts in the grid? Once you've found them all, the remaining letters spell out the punchline to the joke below.

```
F E D A N I O H S A B K
O C P U L L A P O H C C
C N W G K A E R O D J I
U A R R R K I D U U U K
S L E H I A N H J M U J
O A S R O O P I C N A O
D B T O W L T P G I M S
N S L K B S D F L U A S
E A E T U I U S S E E T
K A L E V E R A G E C A
T I P P O N H H S U P N
O P S S S E N M L A C C
W O R H T K A R A T E E
```

BALANCE
BASHO
CALMNESS
CHOP
DAN
FOCUS
GRAPPLE
HOLDS
IPPON
JUDO
JUJITSU
KARATE
KENDO
KICK

KUNG FU
LEVERAGE
OBI
PULL
PUSH
SAMURAI
STANCE
STRIKE
SUMO
TAE KWON DO
TAI CHI
THROW
WRESTLE

What do martial artists like to eat?

_ _ _ _ _ _ _ _ _ _ _ _ !

59
Mountain Wildlife

Lots of animals live in the mountains, and some of them are hiding in the grid. if you find them all, the leftover letters will spell out the answer to this joke: **Why is it hard to carry on a conversation with a goat?**

```
R E V A E B B E C A
U L R E G D A B S E
T E C O U G A R M H
R S K N U M P I H C
R A C C O O N E E O
D E E R B K Y L R Y
U W R B I O O E M O
R O A A G V B U L T
E X B W H S S C O E
H N W I O K H M A A
P Y Y S R L R R B T
O L U A N A F T E T
G I T N M G C I N W
```

BADGER	HARE
BEAR	LYNX
BEAVER	MARMOT
BIGHORN	MINK
BOBCAT	MUSKRAT
CARIBOU	RACCOON
CHIPMUNK	SHREW
COUGAR	VOLE
COYOTE	WEASEL
DEER	WOLF
GOPHER	

_____ _____

____ _____

_____ ___!

60
Feeling Tired

The words below are words that mean TIRED. Find them all in the grid before you feel the same way.

EXHAUSTED   WIPED OUT

FATIGUED   WORN OUT

SHATTERED

```
T N G P F X R I N S
U A R I N S O A E R
O S H A T T E R E D
N D E T S U A H X E
R I N A S O E H R I
O A T U O D E P I W
W E F A T I G U E D
```

61
Shoe Shopping

This man is on a shopping spree for shoes. Help him out by finding all the listed types of shoe in the grid. Be careful, though, because one of the types of shoe in the list can't be found in the grid. Which one is it?

```
M O C C A S I N S D
S E L U M B S U S R
D R S S A F E E L S
B O L L R O C E L
T A L I U H H L E I
  T D E P N S C S O H N
    E N T F D S T R M G H G
      I L A F L N I L R H R S G B
A T R I U I S L O A N N I O E O C I A
P U M P S T D A P R N T I P A B F N H C
G N M K S O T S R E T I A P N U T A G K
E S E O H S E O T P E E P E     A C O S
E S P A D R I L L E S D R R     L A O L
S R E K A E N S I T E N S       P A R E
```

BALLET FLATS   PLATFORM SHOES

CLOGS   PUMPS

ESPADRILLES   SANDALS

FLIP-FLOPS   SLINGBACKS

HIGH HEELS   SLIPPERS

LOAFERS   SNEAKERS

MOCCASINS   STILETTOS

MULES   TENNIS SHOES

PEEP-TOE SHOES   THONGS

The type of shoe that can't be found in the grid is _____!

62
Piggy in the Middle

Hidden in the first grid there are five words related to PIGS. In the second grid are five words beginning with the letters IN, and in the third grid there are five words related to the MIDDLE. See if you can find them all.

PIGGY

A	L	L	U	P	Q	E	S
A	E	A	R	I	S	N	K
A	E	L	E	R	O	N	I
K	N	S	E	U	I	O	A
N	E	L	T	O	Q	R	I
I	N	A	S	O	T	S	E
P	R	E	T	T	O	R	T
U	R	I	A	E	L	N	S

IN

A	T	H	X	E	D	N	I
I	I	N	D	E	E	D	F
H	N	X	A	T	T	A	E
L	C	C	E	T	A	A	E
C	L	N	L	A	L	T	E
H	A	E	I	I	F	L	N
T	E	C	D	A	N	I	N
E	L	T	A	H	I	E	I

THE MIDDLE

R	M	U	I	D	E	M	S
T	L	C	H	U	Y	F	H
W	I	R	N	S	T	C	A
A	L	N	R	A	E	I	L
N	S	E	S	N	E	T	F
A	E	C	T	I	D	M	W
B	B	E	L	R	D	I	A
N	R	A	S	T	E	E	Y

63
Spring Flowers

All these springtime words can be found four times in the puzzle. Can you find all 24 words?

CROCUS

DAFFODIL

HYACINTH

IRIS

PRIMROSE

TULIP

E	H	T	N	I	C	A	Y	H	T	U	L	I	P
C	R	O	C	U	S	H	T	N	I	C	A	Y	H
H	E	L	P	R	I	M	R	O	S	E	E	N	E
Y	E	N	I	R	O	P	T	E	N	H	E	A	P
A	E	D	I	D	I	C	E	U	Y	E	L	L	R
C	S	S	A	L	O	S	U	A	L	I	N	I	I
I	O	S	U	F	O	F	C	S	D	I	C	D	M
N	R	T	U	R	F	I	F	O	A	R	P	O	R
T	M	S	M	C	N	O	F	A	O	I	I	F	O
H	I	I	I	T	O	F	D	C	D	S	L	F	S
E	R	R	H	R	A	R	U	I	N	E	U	A	E
P	P	I	A	D	I	S	C	T	L	E	T	D	A

64
Extinct Animals

All of these creatures are now extinct. Solve the puzzle by finding their names in the grid.

AMMONITE
APATOSAURUS
AUROCHS
CAVE BEAR
DINORNIS
DINOSAUR
DIPLODOCUS
DIRE WOLF
DODO
ELEPHANT BIRD
EOHIPPUS
GIANT ELK
GLYPTODON
GREAT AUK
GROUND SLOTH
HOMO HABILIS
IGUANODON
MAMMOTH
MASTODON
MOA
NEANDERTHAL
PLATYGONUS
PLESIOSAUR
PTERODACTYL
SABER-TOOTH CAT
STEGODON
STEGOSAURUS

TASMANIAN TIGER
THYLACINE

TITANIS
TRICERATOPS

TRILOBITE
VELOCIRAPTOR

```
F P T E R O D A C T Y L W F R H
K E M K N O D O N A U G I E T H
U T A W S T E G O D O N G O E O
A I S F E U E V A E S I L D D M
T N T U Y E R U C S T S I I R O
A O O I C K R U E N D N R V A H
E M D E B O S L A N O E E S E A
R M O W C I D I U S W L E G B B
G A N H N C N O A O O F E L E I
P D S A S A R U L C E G L Y V L
L R T A M G R F I P T E E P A I
A I P S B S Y R E C I L R T C S
T B A L U E A N E D B D B O S P
Y T S R E P R E L I O N E D G O
G N C S T S P T K V L D R O I T
O A I O E N I I O F I L O N A A
N H R S R E W O H O R I H N N R
U P Y S U R U A S O T A P A T E
S E H T O M M A M A E H O E E C
C L D I N O R N I S U L C M L I
N E A N D E R T H A L R S A K R
R E N I C A L Y H T G M B E T T
```

65
Hey Presto!

Look for all these things connected to being a magician in the top hat. If you find them all, the leftover letters will spell out a joke!

BALLS
BOX
CARDS
CLOAK
COIN
CUPS
DOVE
EGG
FUN
PAPER
PIGEON

RABBIT
RINGS
ROPE
SCARF
SPELLS
STAGE
STAR
STRING
WAND
WATCH

```
C S R A B B I T
G O P H O O W G
N D I E O X G W
I I T N L E C C
R I N G S L H E
T S F D O R S D
S U R A T S H N
N S K I N C K A
T C T R T E S W
A A W A E I L T
H R W S G P L E
R O P E F C P U E A P V S A
S D R A C N U D S B P O O R
C E R O R S C N O E G I P D
```

____ __ _____ _____ ____?

____ ____ _____!

66
Cats

Cats are great fun! Can you find all these cat-related words in the grid?

AGILE	CUTE	NAP	STRAY
BASKET	FELINE	NINE LIVES	STROKE
BLACK	FLUFFY	PAWS	TABBY
BRUSH	GINGER	PEDIGREE	TAIL
CAT FOOD	GROOM	PURR	TOMCAT
CATERWAUL	KITTEN	PUSS	TONGUE
CATNIP	LICK	SCRATCH	TOY
CLAWS	LITTER BOX	SLEEP	WHISKERS
CUSHION	MEOW	SOFT	

```
V X D D D N H N D N H M H N Y E D R A B
I L I T T E R B O X E C N S T R O K E R
E A R S J T P K J E I L T B C S S U P U
T I M A Y T C E N I L E F A E U C D T S
O N G B R I P C D H S I O S R A T O E H
Y V B G L K A A A I L N W K T C M E R S
E A E I O T W S N O G A A E Y C S E D E
T U D L N M H R N M P R R T A I S O A V
F S G I N O I H S U C W E T H T O E R I
R L P N O R S O F T A K M E A F A E N L
R E U E O A K I L U S C O O T G G I M E
U E E F D T E R L A T A N A O N I E L N
P P I E F S R L O M H L C U I R O L A I
R S T R A Y S W A L C B E G N W G I E N
```

67
In the Garden

Can you find all of these things you might find in a garden in the watering can?

```
                    E L B A T
                  K S B U S H D
                X S           P R A
          M A                     A I
          C R                     I T B
          G I                       B H
E         O N I A T N U O F L C G R
L S       I O R I N E O L I G N C R
C L R     T Y S U N D I A L I O A T O Y S E
Y U A X   L B T B N O R M W N K M H O R B
C G O D M   T U N U I I E S E E P E H N A
I F   T Y S   E G A T R C W P T L G R A R
B   L B T     S K A T E B O A R D O D B
              S G P I E T N M E E E N E
              P A N G E R D R N H E S C
              A E A I B O F I S W L T U
              D T M F W A E L C D A N E
              E E S O H S R H Y S I L O
```

ANT	FOUNTAIN	LAWN MOWER	SPADE
BARBECUE	FOX	PATH	SUNDIAL
BEE	GATE	PATIO	SWING
BICYCLE	GNOME	POND	TABLE
BIRD	GRASS	SHED	TOYS
BUSH	HEDGEHOG	SKATEBOARD	TREE
BUTTERFLY	HOSE	SLUG	
FLOWER	LADYBUG	SNAIL	

68
Dogs

Dogs are man's best friend. Find all the doggy words in the grid below.

AFFECTIONATE
BARK
BEG
BISCUIT
BONE
BREEDER
BULLDOG
CHEW
COLLAR
COMPANION
EXERCISE
FAITHFUL
FETCH
FIDO
GUARD DOG
GUIDE DOG
HOUND
KEEN NOSE
LEASH
MONGREL
MUTT
PAWS
PLAYFUL
POOCH
RETRIEVER
SCOTTIE
SHEEPDOG

G	K	B	E	G	E	S	C	O	T	T	I	E	C
U	V	E	X	M	N	S	N	N	M	S	P	A	H
I	N	P	E	S	L	R	I	A	T	L	N	A	E
D	E	T	A	N	O	I	T	C	E	F	F	A	W
E	W	I	K	W	N	R	A	Y	R	S	I	T	G
D	A	U	F	C	S	O	M	T	F	E	S	A	O
O	L	C	O	N	I	R	S	A	R	T	X	S	D
G	K	S	O	I	A	T	I	E	A	R	T	E	P
V	A	I	W	L	F	T	S	Y	E	N	R	I	E
S	A	B	L	E	H	T	Y	V	E	N	O	B	E
L	R	O	T	F	N	M	E	I	H	C	S	L	H
L	C	C	U	E	A	I	H	K	O	S	U	B	S
E	H	L	E	T	R	R	P	M	R	F	A	R	N
R	E	M	U	T	T	R	P	O	Y	A	A	E	I
G	F	L	E	S	E	A	I	A	O	C	B	E	L
N	I	R	D	T	N	R	L	E	A	C	N	D	P
O	D	I	E	I	S	P	L	M	R	H	H	E	A
M	O	T	O	U	G	O	D	L	L	U	B	R	Y
A	R	N	F	F	I	N	S	E	H	O	U	N	D
N	I	S	Y	G	U	A	R	D	D	O	G	E	O

SNIFF	TAIL		WOOF
STAY	TERRIER		YAP
STICK	WALK		YELP

69
How Do You Feel Today?

Hidden in the grid are seven words related to being grumpy and seven words related to being happy—when you find them, write the **happy words** on the smiley face and the **grumpy ones** on the frowning face. When you've found all seven of one kind, that's how you will be feeling today.

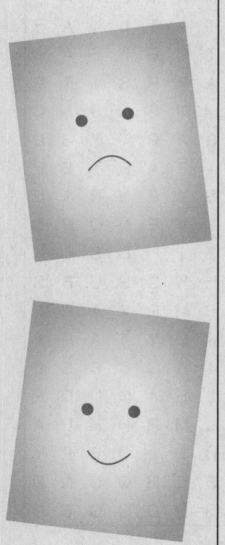

```
P B W M Y L L O J J S S S C
U A S P O A I S O L A B H O
U N I S O A A T E D L R M M
I G N E E A N P S O T R F P
I R E L N H C H E E R F U L
D Y U A N I S E O C D R T A
I E A B G E H L G N M S O I
R T T I A R E W P W H N U N
E C Y H D L A T N E T N O C
S R R A G O I T T E N A R S
E O R I L I T G I M F A R B
D E E C D N L R H F S R U I
E O M T E P A E L N I R E C
Y I S O A T Y E D T C E I D
O L R G N M E I A S A T D H
N E O U T S R B N E A A B I
N L P S U W L O E T C D T R
A F A O N E I E S S L O G M
H T R U A R E C N I S Y E O
C G D A L R E T P N I E A B
```

70
Ball Games

You need a ball to play all the sports listed below. One of the words is hidden **TEN** times in the grid, but the others appear only once. Can you find them all?

CRICKET
FOOTBALL
GOLF
HOCKEY
RUGBY
SOCCER
SQUASH
TENNIS

```
Q A I N A E R I N E T R A E
R S Q U A S H C I N E A S T
E H T Y B G U R R C F U R I
A E E N S O T E C I R L A I
N S N G E L T O Y A C B O F
R H N U O F S I E E N K O G
S A I T Y L E R I N K O E E
A S S G O L F T R I T C F T
E H O U F F L A N B S L O E
C L R T L I O A A B O E N H
F S K O O R G L T G F L O G
I A G E G H L N Y U E C S R
```

71
Round Things

Find all the round things in the grid.

BALL
BOTTLE CAP
CD DISC
FRISBEE
HULA-HOOP
MARBLE

MOON
PLANET
PIPE
RING
WHEEL

```
        B P
    U G F A W H
  P C E L C L U M
  L D L E E R L O
N A D B E L E A O S
G N I R B T E H N R
  E S A S T P O W
  T C M I O I O I
    N S R B P P
        F T
```

72
Feeling Hungry?

Find all the listed foods in the doughnut. Doesn't it make you hungry?

```
            J U I
        N E K C I H C
      I S B T P U G Y N D I
    L P A O I I O D N N S R T
    I I N R Z C D N N O W Y E U T
    H A R Z E T A D L M A S G E O
  C N A A C O C S W E E T S R E M I
  A C C R H N T           L E J U G A I
N R Y E O O S             R E B N T I L
P E A R T O L             M L M A O T G
E M D T R M K             E L A R B P D
S O O N E R I             S L Y H O U I
C E I U E B T E T A L O C O H C E
  B E A G L W L S P N N R G I S
  O R H A H P A C H E R R I E S
    T E C Y N P R E D A L A S
    C A K E U A T P D S L
      D R G T E S N
        M S I
```

APPLE

BANANA

BREAD

CAKE

CARROT

CHEESE

CHERRIES

CHICKEN

CHIPS

CHOCOLATE

COOKIES

COTTON CANDY

DOUGHNUT

GRAPES

HAMBURGER

HOT DOG

ICE CREAM

JELLY

LEMON

LIME

ORANGE

PEAR

PEAS

PIE

PIZZA

SALAD

STRAWBERRY

SWEETS

TOMATO

WATERMELON

Taste Test

The food on the previous page has definitely given me an apetite.
Find all the words relcted to food in the grid below

APPETIZING
AROMATIC
ATTRACTIVE
BITTER
DELECTABLE
DELICIOUS
EDIBLE
ENJOYABLE
EXOTIC
FINGER-LICKING
LIP-SMACKING
LUSCIOUS
MOREISH
MOUTHWATERING
NICE
PALATABLE
PIQUANT
PLEASANT
PLEASURE
RELISH
SALTY
SAVORY
SCRUMPTIOUS
SENSATION
SOUR
SPICY
SWEET

```
Y G N A T G N I T P M E T G S
Y J E L P Y R O V A S N N E X
T S L I Q P H D F H A I N D M
S A B P S W E E T S K S K G O
A L A S W H D T A C A R R N R
T T T M N I C E I T S E Z I E
F Y A A D N L L I Z T R M L I
H O L C D P R O N T I O R A S
S O A K E E N D I Y U N E E H
U R P I G N L B E T M L G P P
O P K N H E R I H L B M E P L
I E I G R E L W C A B X U A E
C F O Q L O A B Y I O I R Y A
S N E I U T F O A T O B D R S
U W S R E A J E I T S U O E U
L H U R E N N C I D C P S V R
R O I F E N E T O D H E I A E
S N A R O M A T I C O R L C E
G N E E V I T C A R T T A E Y
O S C R U M P T I O U S D A D
```

TANGY   TO DIE FOR   ZEST

TASTY   VERY APPEALING

TEMPTING   YUMMY

74
Play the Game

Would you like to be an athlete?
Can you find all these sports hidden in the grid?

ARCHERY
ATHLETICS
BASEBALL
BASKETBALL
CRICKET
CYCLING
FOOTBALL
GOLF
HIKING
HOCKEY
HURDLING
JOGGING
KARTING
MOTOCROSS
NETBALL
POLO
RACING
RIDING
RUGBY
RUNNING
SHOOTING
SKATING
SURFING
SWIMMING
WALKING
YACHTING

```
        G Y G A Q L
      N R O T O L O P
      I E L H B R U G B Y
    K H F L Y A C H T I N G
    I C B E A S S O R C O T O M
  H R N T E B K K G K L G H J G H
  A U I I R T A E N A L N O P N O
  L C R D F E T T I R A I C Y I D
  S L T D I N I B K T B G K Z N G
  G W A E L N N A L I E G E K N S
  R N I B K I G L A N S O Y I U V
  A I M T C N L W G A J T R R
    C L M O I G M T B O F C
    I C I O R X G O I S
    N Y N F C H N U
      G C G S G W
```

Baddies

Can you find all the criminals in the grid? When you've found them all, write out the leftover letters from top to bottom in the spaces below to spell out a joke and its punchline.

R	E	G	R	O	F	W	H	A	L
T	D	R	E	T	S	B	O	M	A
G	O	O	T	N	H	I	E	T	D
M	U	G	G	E	R	V	C	E	N
E	T	H	S	U	E	I	T	B	A
A	L	T	T	Q	V	A	U	A	V
F	A	O	N	N	R	R	R	D	D
R	W	L	O	I	G	U	N	D	U
C	U	C	P	L	A	H	H	I	A
A	M	S	A	E	O	L	B	E	R
U	R	R	T	D	N	O	L	E	F
H	O	O	D	L	U	M	T	I	G
C	R	O	O	K	E	L	A	E	V
R	E	B	B	O	R	R	R	S	R

BADDIE
BURGLAR
CONVICT
CROOK
DELINQUENT
FELON
FORGER

FRAUD
HOODLUM
LOOTER
MOBSTER
MUGGER
OUTLAW
PIRATE

ROBBER
RUSTLER
THUG
VANDAL
VILLAIN

_____ __ _____ ____ ____

_____?

_____!

76
Happy

Can you find the listed happy words in the grid? When you've found them all, write out the leftover letters from top to bottom in the spaces below the grid to spell the answer to the joke.

```
J O Y O U S I S E D B U O Y A N T S C B
R E P P I H C M E E T D S Q D N U I L
B E A M I N G I L L U F L A E I A O T I
B L I S S F U L G I C U F Y L T R R A T
H E A R T E N E D G F O O U G G E U T H
T N E I L L U B E H N J N R H C B T S E
C I R O H P U E T T R I A T H C U P C X
Y L B B U B L R E E G T C E E C X A E U
E L A T E D I E V D I E E I H N E R N L
Y L L O J M H O A F A R N I O R T I D T
J U B I L A N T I S F T R I O J R E S A
T N A I D A R E W U E P A L A G E L D N
L A I V O J D O L W Y D D E L L I R H T
```

BEAMING	CHIRPY	EUPHORIC	GRIN	OVERJOYED
BLISSFUL	CHUFFED	EXUBERANT	HEARTENED	PLEASED
BLITHE	CONTENTED	EXULTANT	JOLLY	RADIANT
BUBBLY	DELIGHTED	GENIAL	JOVIAL	RAPTUROUS
BUOYANT	EBULLIENT	GLAD	JOYOUS	REJOICING
CHEERFUL	ECSTATIC	GLEE	JUBILANT	SMILE
CHIPPER	ELATED	GRATIFIED	MIRTHFUL	THRILLED

Did you hear the joke about the huge Easter egg?

_ _ ' _   _ _ _ _ _   _ _ _ _   _ _   _ _ _ _ _ _ _ !

Something Sweet

See if you can find all these sweet treats hidden in the grid.

APPLE TURNOVER
BANANA SPLIT
BISCUIT
BLANCMANGE
BUTTERSCOTCH
CARAMEL
CHEESECAKE
CHOCOLATE
COOKIE
CUSTARD PIE
DOUGHNUT
ECLAIR
FRUIT SALAD
FUDGE
GINGERBREAD
HONEYCOMB
ICE CREAM
JELLY
LOLLIPOP
MARZIPAN
MERINGUE
MOUSSE
MUFFIN
PEACH MELBA
PROFITEROLE
SHERBET

SORBET
SPONGE
SWISS ROLL

SYRUP
TOFFEE
TREACLE

TRIFLE
WAFER
WAFFLE

```
H E T E B R E H S R E F A W V
C J T Z D K L O L L I P O P N
T M Y A B L A N C M A N G E L
O D O N L D N E U G N I R E M
C H V U N O I Y S E Y D M F U
S N I U S P C C S K I A H F F
R S W I S S R O L L R K A O F
E L F I R T E M H A Y B O T I
T S P O N G E B C C L O T O N
T R E V O N R U T E L P P A C
U G N E S D S I M S E W C O T
B F I Y L O O H D T J U N I E
N R R N R C C U T I S S L B K
A U R B G A R R G T O P G I A
P I E I E E E E A H S H C S C
I T W P A A R R T A N E T C E
Z S N A C L D B N I C U E U S
R A I L F P C A R R F G T I E
A L E S I F N E E E D O Y T E
M A O E D A L A A U A T R N H
I D A S B O M E F R E D T P C
```

Zzzzzzz

All the listed words begin with the letter Z. Can you find them all?

ZAMBIA
ZANY
ZAPPER
ZEBRA
ZENITH
ZEST
ZERO
ZIGZAG
ZILLION
ZIMBABWE
ZINC
ZIP
ZITHER
ZIRCON
ZODIAC
ZOMBIE
ZONE
ZOOLOGY
ZOOM
ZULU

S	C	D	W	S	N	S	T	D	L	S	T
H	N	U	R	O	L	Z	S	T	E	C	D
R	I	N	C	A	E	I	I	Z	U	L	U
S	Z	R	E	N	R	M	L	T	T	A	R
Z	I	H	I	U	E	B	N	S	H	A	T
Z	A	T	Y	E	C	A	E	D	L	E	R
O	H	M	C	G	N	B	E	Z	A	P	R
O	S	Y	B	A	T	W	Z	E	R	O	R
M	E	G	M	I	I	E	L	H	U	Z	A
N	S	O	E	C	A	D	D	R	A	T	A
Z	I	L	L	I	O	N	O	N	E	Z	R
L	G	O	N	S	Z	R	Y	Z	I	E	T
A	E	O	P	W	H	O	N	P	P	Y	U
E	C	Z	D	L	S	R	N	P	A	Z	O
I	G	A	Z	G	I	Z	A	E	T	E	E
N	A	R	S	X	X	Z	E	O	I	S	L
T	G	M	E	I	B	M	O	Z	A	T	B

79
Read All about It!

All the words in this word search are
connected with books. Can you find them all in the grid?

AUTHOR
BOOK
CHAPTER
CONTENTS
COVER
FACT
FICTION
HARDBACK
ILLUSTRATION
INDEX
PAGE
PAPERBACK

PRINTER
PUBLISHER
SENTENCE
TITLE
WORD

```
G W V X L S I E L G S E
E S T N E T N O C D I S
I L L U S T R A T I O N
K F T E L P R O H T U A
C K I I A U U I E S K E
A C O C T B A P E D C L
B H R O T L R G I N A N
R A C E B I N D E X B A
E P S O N S O T T O D D
P T R T V H N N F C R I
A E E E L E G A P O A H
P R U A S R R N W S H F
```

80
Mini Word Search

Hidden in the first
grid are five words
that can come after
the word SEA. In the
second grid are five
words that can come
after the word SIDE.
Can you find them all?

SEA _____

```
Z F R G A J X
L I D C Y Q E
E N A L P S E
R M S O R I K
O H R O U C Q
H T H B O K I
S H N V W P T
```

SIDE _____

```
Q O Z R V L S
S A D D L E C
I H M A N A P
M K O I R G B
Y C L W C E J
T I F F X D K
N K C W P U H
```

81
Bad Hair Day

All these faulty words can be found in the grid.

BLEMISHED
BUST
CRACKED
CRUMBLING
CRUSHED
DAMAGED
DEFECTIVE
DEFORMED
DUFF
FAULTY
FRACTURED
FRAGMENTED
HARMED
IMPAIRED
IMPERFECT
INCOMPLETE
INFERIOR

IRREGULAR
KAPUT
REJECT
SCRATCHED
SHATTERED
SHODDY
SMASHED
SNAPPED
SPLINTERED
SPLIT
SUBSTANDARD
SULLIED
TAINTED
TARNISHED
TORN
UNSOUND
WARPED

```
D W V I N C O M P L E T E I
D E R I A P M I R J I O N D
W O M Y O H O A L M G F D E
K A O R A W L N P Y E T E F
D L R R O U O E N R D S G E
O E M P G F R L I R G U A C
B E T E E F E O A N O B M T
D V R N E D R D L N I S A I
O R A C I S N A P P E D D V
I Y T L F A D E H S A M S E
G C N I T R T S S H O D D Y
A D R S T K A D H O N A B D
I N B A L C U C A N S W E O
A U D N C F E I T S R H L O
S O E E F K G J T U S O H G
U S H S R A E N E U R I T N
L N S S C E Y D R R O E A I
L U I L T R T C E N I A D L
I B M S T O A N D E T H F B
E L E I I G N T I A E C A M
D S L K V O R T C L I A U U
E P B T U P A K N H P L L R
S T A R N I S H E D E S T C
D E T N E M G A R F S D Y R
```

82
Tricks and Treats

Can you spot the word in the list that does not appear in the grid?

APPLE
BROOMSTICK
CAPE
CHARM
CLOAK
FAMILIAR
GHOST
GHOUL
GOWN
HALLOWEEN
HAT
HAUNT
MONSTER
MOON
PHANTOM
PUMPKIN
SAINT
SKELETON
SOUL
STARS
SURPRISE
SWEET
TURNIP
WIG
WITCH

```
F H B F E B I E W A S E C R G
I A N S U R P R I S E T E A T
R U M F I E A N G E C R A N I
A N B I N O T E L E K S I R E
L T G N L E O R I A E A P N S
E C L S R I E A O I S K U T E
C L O A K V A W V N C A M T R
S R E O I L P R O I T O P E G
F E T A B H E C T L O N K E R
S T E P A C P S U N L L I W I
O S E N V A M I C L U A N S N
S N T R E O T H N O I S H O A
T O E C O L A R H R A P P L E
M M U R G R H G N M U I S A H
E O B L M T S O H G U T T R N
```

The word that does not appear in the grid is _____!

83
Skipping Game

Which of the skipping words is
hidden ten times?

BOUND
HOP
JUMP
PRANCE
RHYTHM
SPRING
TEMPO
TWIRL

```
H D Y W E T I P B Q P P G U
J U M P E C A O B Z M M I P
Q E X M T E N H U U U R U M
J N P V W I M A J H J X L J
T O P G I H H Q R B O U N D
S O X P R R T A V P M U J D
D P M R L S Y W F J J P U Z
O U R C W L H K U K U U S G
J Y V I L L R M Z Y M F M O
P M U J N P P F C X P M E P
G A S K O G R S M Q Z T J H
J B N T A I W U K V N F C Y
```

84
Candy

```
L A S N E T A L O C O H C A
R I N E A N A U H A G N A N
E T C A I B L O L L I P O P
F U N O A L C S T T G M M P
R T N A R O L E M E T I I O
E E R F L I B E C U N U N P
S B A A N R C I J T G E T I
H R T R E F R E S H E R S L
E E G H O O R T I A B E G L
R H S U C N M S O R T I A O
S S E I M P S E I L L E J L
N U L E S S R A O I T E N A
```

Listed below are 8 candies,
and they can each be found twice
in the grid. Can you find all 16
words?

CHOCOLATE
GUMS
JELLIES
LICORICE
LOLLIPOP
MINTS
REFRESHERS
SHERBET

85
Clumsy

Each of these types of clumsy words can be found three times in the grid. How quickly can you find all 21 words?

ACCIDENT

AWKWARD

FALL

SLIP

STUMBLE

TRIP

UNBALANCE

D	T	C	U	P	B	T	N	E	D	I	C	C	A
R	P	N	I	N	R	E	C	M	L	U	D	T	L
A	S	R	E	T	B	N	I	U	L	L	R	L	L
W	T	T	V	D	A	A	F	N	A	I	A	D	A
K	K	N	U	L	I	A	L	B	P	F	W	F	F
W	Q	Z	A	M	W	C	M	A	Z	J	K	S	G
A	J	B	S	K	B	P	C	L	N	E	W	T	R
T	N	X	W	L	C	L	W	A	X	C	A	U	A
U	S	A	C	C	I	D	E	N	T	S	E	M	L
Y	R	P	I	R	T	P	Y	C	D	L	W	B	S
D	S	T	U	M	B	L	E	E	Q	I	B	L	K
N	O	H	V	U	S	L	I	P	G	P	I	E	F

86
Photography

All these photography words can be found four times in the puzzle. Can you find all 32 words?

CAMERA

DEVELOP

FLASH

FOCUS

FRAME

LENS

SNAP

ZOOM

M	O	O	Z	H	P	R	S	F	F	P	Y	C	D
S	N	A	P	S	B	O	N	U	O	R	A	U	H
Z	O	F	R	A	M	E	L	L	C	M	A	S	X
D	E	V	E	L	O	P	E	E	E	O	A	M	E
S	U	C	O	F	A	V	P	R	V	L	F	F	E
C	S	N	E	L	E	D	A	K	F	E	R	L	M
F	A	U	L	D	M	E	N	G	S	A	D	E	O
M	L	M	C	L	A	V	S	N	M	R	F	N	O
Z	V	A	E	O	R	E	E	E	J	E	O	S	Z
Q	O	N	S	R	F	L	A	S	H	M	C	N	O
W	S	O	S	H	A	O	H	P	T	A	U	A	O
A	R	E	M	A	C	P	A	N	S	C	S	P	M

Building Blocks

Have a go at finding all the listed buildings in the jumbo word search grid.

ABBEY
BANK
BARN
BUNGALOW
CABIN
CAFE
CASTLE
CATHEDRAL
CHALET
CHAPEL
CHURCH
CONVENT
DAIRY
FACTORY
HALL
HOSPITAL
HOTEL
HOUSE
INN
LIBRARY
MANSION
MINT
MUSEUM
OFFICE
RESTAURANT
SALON
SCHOOL
SHED

```
G D D G S I D T O W E R I G K
I W D C T T N E M E N E T I S
Y E B B A E I T G C E D S I E
E P V I T S R E E I A S S L S
Y C N E I U T D L L U F Y A P
R N I G O O C L N P A R E T O
M Y I F N H C O E T A H H I R
S R A K F H E R N R O O C P T
U I R N U O M A B V T E A S S
I A E R L A R I P E E S W O C
S D C G R U L O L E D N R H E
A H F K A C L O O H C S T A N
L N E T H R A M A N S I O N T
O T S A I S A T E S L O Y G E
N E P P M H L C H N U A R R R
R E E O N E I L I E S Y O B E
L O D H A D L B A V D T T A R
M U E S U M A T P H N R C R N
I E A S O C R E T I U B A N K
B U N G A L O W M L I G F L N
```

SHOP
SPORTS CENTER
STATION
SUPERMARKET

TENEMENT
TOWER
VICARAGE

88
Feeling Peckish

Find all the "eating" words in the grid, then write the leftover letters in the spaces below to spell out a joke and its punchline.

BANQUET
BREAKFAST
CHOMP
CONSUME
DEMOLISH
DEVOUR
DINE
FEAST
FEED
GOBBLE
GOLLOP
GORGE
GUZZLE
INGEST
LUNCH
MUNCH
PACK AWAY
PARTAKE
RELISH
SAVOR
SCOFF
SHOVEL DOWN

SNACK
STUFF
SWALLOW
TUCK IN

W	H	E	M	U	S	N	O	C	A	T	T	D	I
S	H	O	V	E	L	D	O	W	N	D	E	T	H
E	E	G	G	T	S	A	E	F	G	G	U	G	S
S	A	R	H	Y	S	A	V	O	R	P	Q	O	T
T	O	I	C	S	O	D	L	N	M	H	N	B	U
G	P	I	N	S	W	L	E	O	I	B	A	B	F
F	A	A	U	G	O	O	H	M	R	K	B	L	F
R	C	R	M	P	E	C	L	E	O	I	C	E	E
K	K	U	N	E	D	S	A	L	H	L	K	U	E
A	A	O	L	R	N	K	T	S	A	A	I	D	T
D	W	V	A	U	F	I	C	N	T	W	Y	S	G
E	A	E	O	A	N	O	D	R	O	D	S	Y	H
E	Y	D	S	O	F	C	A	H	S	I	L	E	R
F	L	T	K	F	S	P	H	G	U	Z	Z	L	E

____ ___ ___ ___ ___

__ ___ _____?

_____ ___ ____ _____!

89
Supermarket Sweep

See if you can find all of these shop-related words in the grid.

ASSISTANT
BAR CODE
BASKET
CARRIER BAG
CART
CASH
CHECKOUT
CHILLER CABINET
CREDIT CARD
CUSTOMER
FREE DELIVERY
FREEZER

```
F T N A T S I S S A G Y V T Z U G
R O O R L U P H N A S O Y P D O D
E L A G M N E E B S O T L I P C R
E C H I L L E R C A B I N E T H A
D R H U F N E F S I O D N C E E C
E T E L G I N M R R A I S E K C T
L D O M R T I P E E N L H R S K I
I N O R O M A N A G E R O Y A O D
V U A C D T N L T S O Z E F B U E
E C I T R A S I N A S O E N F T R
R I L T C A M U C A S H G R I E C
Y M A S B E B D C R E K C A P L R
```

LINE
MANAGER
OPENING TIME
PACKER
RECEIPT
SCANNER
SHELF
SPECIAL OFFER

90
Word Search Race

All of these listed words can follow SNOW, like man in snowman. To solve the puzzle, you need a friend, a brother, or a sister! One of you has the words on the left and one has the words on the right. Take turns searching for one of your words—but there is a thirty-second time limit for each turn (the other person must time their opponent while they search). The first person to find all their words is the winner! Remember: you mustn't peek at the grid while the other person is taking their turn to search.

BALL		BANK
BEAR		BERRY
BLADING		BLIND
BLOWER		BOARD
BOOT		BOUND
BUNTING		BUTTERCUP
CAP		CHAIN
CONE		DRIFT
DROP		FALL
FIELD		FINCH
FLAKE		FLURRY
GOGGLES		GOOSE
GUARD		HOLE
HUT		LEOPARD
LINE		MAN
MOBILE		PLOW
SCENE		SHOE
STORM		SUIT
TIRE		WHITE

```
E S E L G G O G S H F I E L D
R S Y M S L S I C A M S K D T
I D R I F T E N I A E G B R N
T B Y H E G I O C S O A E A I
T O E N O F N A P O R N R U S
R O E E L L I I S A A T R G M
A T A U O E E D M R C Y P N
E R R B L H H L S A I D U T E
B R B L P A S I N D L C R E I
Y S A O H U T B A T R B Y B E
C F R W A N M O E E A O I O S
A K H E E R O M T N M T P U T
R E N R E D D T K A O R I N I
L P T F N P U S W O E C O D U
C E N I L B U N T I N G D T S
T R L O H A N I A H C A N C S
I B W E S W K L B A L L A O G
M E N E C S H E T U A P R E N
```

91
Ancient Egypt

See if you can find all of these Egyptology words in the pyramid-shaped grid. We've put one in to help get you started. If you look carefully, you can find another related word hiding somewhere in the grid.

GIZA
HATHOR
HATSHEPSUT
HIEROGLYPH
HORUS
HOWARD CARTER

ISIS
KARNAK
MEMNON
MUT
NEFERTITI
OBELISK
PAPYRUS
PHARAOH
PYRAMID
RAMESES
SARCOPHAGUS
STELA
TEMPLE
THUTMOSIS
TOMB
TREASURE
TUTANKHAMUN
VALLEY OF THE KINGS

ABU SIMBEL
ABYDOS
AFRICA
AKHENATEN
ALEXANDRIA
AMENHOTEP
AMUN-RA
ANUBIS
APIS
CARTOUCHE
CLEOPATRA
DYNASTY
EDFU
EGYPT

```
                    R
                  V S P
                A A A T C
                K L I R E
              V S L E S N L
            M Z I E K X I U A
            Q Y L Y A H A S M
          P C H E O R K U N M A
          H A P B F N G H U D K
        S A R Y O T A U M E F R J
        I R T L A H K M M G N D I
      A B A O G P E Y A L A S A E A
      B U O U O H K D C E D H U T T
    A Y N H C R A I E I B Y M K R E F
    Z D A R H E T N L R M N R E N Y N
  B I O A I E I H G P F I A A A M A P T
  M G S U R O H O S M A S S R D M N T A
  H O W A R D C A R T E R U T P Y G E O U P
  I T I T R E F E N N T R B Y O A P I S N T
T U S P E H S T A H U E E A M E N H O T E P B
T H U T M O S I S M A R T A P O E L C X L S S
```

92
Ice...

All the words in this puzzle can follow the word ICE. Do you think you can crack it?

```
F X S S S T B U C K E T L R M S T R I R
S L T R I E S T Y E L R A G M I N B E O
K S B O A T T R F T X I N E L B R A N H
S C E O D D R T I H O A D E L E L G N C
M M I L D L O C S C B S O R A T G O I N
A A E P E P H N K A Y Y U K E N D L C A
S I C R A O I T A Y E E E N I A R S F K
F D E H O I L T T G M R K C E E U L B A
D N N R I H S U I I O T N C E P A L N C
R E I U S N O A N T K A C Y O R I N K U
E D L R O G E N G C D R M I S H A H P B
E O A U T B R N A Q E Q E A I L P O S E
O E D G T R F P A A N I E S L O P G M H
T U A R E E N I M E S U O H Y S E O D A
```

AGE	BUCKET	LAND
ANCHOR	COLD	MACHINE
BLOCK	CREAM	PACK
BLUE	CUBE	PICK
BOAT	DANCING	POP
BOUND	FIELD	RINK
BOX	HOCKEY	SKATING
BREAKER	HOUSE	YACHT

```
S E L A C S M Y F I G
M E L E W O T D N A H
I S O A P D I S H N E
E L T S N R T A I T G
E N I A I H E U T O N
Y N L E B T R W B O O
K C E D Y O L R O T P
G E S M R L I N O H S
E R A R D C P O T B S
F A I R N E I E L R E
A M A N U C P S E U O
D I R T A A I A G S A
N C E L L F G U T H N
M R U B B E R D U C K
```

Bath...

Can you find all of these bathroom items in the top grid?

CERAMIC	SCALES
DRAIN	SHOWER
FACE CLOTH	SINK
HAND TOWEL	SOAP DISH
LAUNDRY BIN	SPONGE
MIRROR	TAP
ROBE	TILES
RUBBER DUCK	TOOTHBRUSH
RUG	TUB

...Time

Have you got enough time to find all of these words in the bottom grid?

ALARM	PRESS
BELL	RADIO
BLEEP	RINGING
BUTTON	SECOND
BUZZER	SLEEP
CLOCK	SNOOZE
HOUR	SWITCH OFF
MINUTE	TIME
MORNING	WINDUP

```
K A A P U D N I W A O
S L E E P T H S A I D
P G T D I A N S D E N
R T N M R O A A B M O
E R E I O U R H U R C
S E M Z G R O S T A E
S A E I T N N H T L S
E C D L N R I I O A B
R G M I E U N R N L E
A S O Z T R T L E G F
I E Z L H A N E L S E
O U C D R T P I A E E
B S W I T C H O F F B
L K C O L C G N M S K
```

95
SSSSnakes...

See if you can spot all of these snakes hiding in the grid. Be extra careful, as five of them can be found twice in the grid.

ADDER
ANACONDA
ASP
BOA CONSTRICTOR
COBRA
COPPERHEAD
CORAL SNAKE
KING SNAKE
MAMBA
PYTHON
RATTLESNAKE
SERPENT
SIDEWINDER
TREE SNAKE
VIPER

```
G W L L G M I L H A R B O C
I Y T N E P R E S L G M I I
B O A C O N S T R I C T O R
V L A H S A I L G C M D S O
T I I R B E W H O Y E A L S
E O P M B I T R V I P E R E
S K A E E O A O P I A H L T
G M A M R L C B Y E S R C N
H S I N S O T E T V P E L N
R R E N S I S O H T Y P E C
D A A L R G G N O M E P I S
H K T E O T N R N K N O S E
E A B T I L S I A W O C I E
A C D T L R A N K N I E D S
N D L O G E S M H A D D E R
O T N A R E S E N I Y S W E
H O C O L D A N L R T N I I
T E A T C B S A A O R E N T
Y H T L I A D G N K M A D E
P A C D S D N V O R E T E I
R A E N E L S A R E O P R A
W T I R H E K A N S E E R T
```

The five snakes that can be found twice in the grid are _____, _____, _____, _____, and _____!

Cat Nap

```
P S T R E E T O P J Q
E W Y I N B E N A C V
T I R X I C C A B D E
S T H V H U N B T C Y
R L F H S O X O E W O
O F L H N F Q I K A U
O Y I I U Z P L N R R
D O U R S L E E A D P
N L S S E W J R L R I
U P O T H S O K B O L
Z F N M T E I D G B L
A A O N N G L D N E O
M S T A I R S F E I W
E S U O H N E E R G W
```

Can you spot all of these places where cats like to sleep in the top grid?

BLANKET	SHELF
CUSHION	SOFA
DOORSTEP	STAIRS
FIRESIDE	TREETOP
GREENHOUSE	WARDROBE
IN THE SUNSHINE	WINDOWSILL
MANTELPIECE	YOUR PILLOW
ON A BOILER	

Doggy Bag

See if you can find all of these types of bags in the bottom grid.

BRIEFCASE	POUCH
CARRIER BAG	RUCKSACK
DUFFEL BAG	SCHOOL BAG
GRIP	SHOPPING BAG
HANDBAG	SHOULDER BAG
HAVERSACK	TOILETRY BAG
KNAPSACK	VANITY CASE
MAKEUP BAG	

```
M Y D U F F E L B A G
G A B R E I R R A C V
S H O U L D E R B A G
H K T N T G E L N R N
O M C T E A D I B U I
P G N A S B T P R C G
P A K E S Y I O I K A
I B C H C R L T E S B
N P A A G T E R F A L
G U S N I E H V C C O
B E P D E L C N A K O
A K A B S I U O S H H
G A N A T O O Y E E C
D M K G L T P R M I S
```

98
Toolbox

Can you find all of the listed tools in the toolbox-shaped grid?

ALLEN WRENCH CROWBAR NAIL GUN SHOVEL
BLOWTORCH DRILL PINCERS SPANNER
BRACKET FILE PLIERS TSQUARE
CHISEL HAMMER RULER TWEEZERS
CLAMP MALLET SCREWDRIVER VICE

```
G F Z Q D O G O T D O T U I N O T E L I F
D R G I N A O T F I U A N S O D T I A B G
N A                                   M S
K B     If you look carefully, you can find another tool    O E
T W          hiding somewhere in the grid.          R C
I A O P P N U E D S H R A O I T E N A A L W S
E B R O L I T G M A E F A B B E A D U A N A R
H R C E S I U I M L L O L T L L E Q M P A S N
R A E I V S E M U N L O A E L O S P T E D K M
R C G N M I E R U V I C E E S T W I S A K C A
H K E O U R R G S T R R N N E I A T B I P A L
S E O E D T L D R F D W A N I E H S O L O H L
G T M H T I U A W R R E N I S E O C C R D A E
L R S P A N N E R E T P T W E E Z E R S C N T
I E A N B S O R N S R E C N I P E T H L U H I
G N M A E C D C S V K C O R T I A E N F L S R
L E V O H S H E O P A T S I H N U E C D L S R
```

The hidden tool in the grid is _____ !

99
Art Attack

Can you find all of the listed artists' materials in the grid?

```
E Y F H S U R B T N I A P R K L A H C
S H P X Y P A I T D F D R E N N I H T
E A C R D O G N P A I N T B O X Y L S
U D B A I T T K N U O G F M D N E K V
L P E L U M S N L E P C A U O S E R L
B O V Y E O A F I A I B R I A T E A I
T S D A G B G R L A R S L E C M R W O
L T N S R N R E Y O P I T H D E A S D
A E O T I N T U W C M L P N P N P I E
B R I K U T I N S R O A I M R O U E E
O P S E E B O S E H D L E O N U U N S
C A L S E C E V H A W T O G E L B N N
M I U C H G R A P H I T E R G D T A I
F N M R A E P R U S S I A N B L U E L
S T E N C I L L E E H W R O L O C S O
```

BROWN OCHRE	GRAPHITE	POT	THINNER
BURNT SIENNA	INK	PRIMARY COLOR	TUBE
CHALK	LINSEED OIL	PRUSSIAN BLUE	UMBER
COBALT BLUE	MASKING FLUID	RAW SIENNA	UNDERCOAT
COLOR WHEEL	OIL PAINT	SABLE BRUSH	VARNISH
EASEL	PAINTBOX	SKETCHPAD	VERMILION
EMULSION	PAINTBRUSH	SPONGE	
GLUE	PALETTE	STENCIL	
GOUACHE	POSTER PAINT	TEMPERA	

How Do You Feel Today?

Hidden in the grid are seven words related to feeling light and seven words related to feeling heavy—when you find them, write the **light words** on the smiley face and the **heavy words** on the frowning face. When you've found all seven of one type, that's how you will be feeling today.

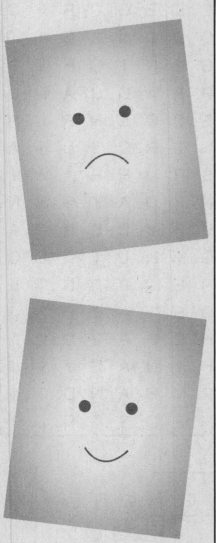

```
C K W V E N N S C R N S O U
R G N S E L H E F T Y O T P
C R A H N S B O T A R H U E
N S T O D A T A E C R A G M
I I N E A E P S T O T R D R
L F I E H U L A N R S D E E
O C D R T I A I B E O L D G
N M N I M B L E C S K P A O
R M T I A E P W H A N U O E
C A D L S R A O I T T E L N
A S R S E O I L T Y G E M F
Y S M I L F A B T E C D P N
R I H S U B I H O T E O P V
A V L N U R G E I S N O A T
E E C L D I L R G D N M I S
A K K H E E O U E T R E N E
A Y B W I L A R P S W L O E
C D T R F A O I N I E I S L
O G M H T U U A R R E G N I
Y S E O S C D A L Y R A T P
```

101
Down on the Farm

See if you can find all the farm-related words in the grid. The words are on the next page. Once you've done that, write out the leftover letters from top to bottom in the spaces below to spell out a joke and its punchline.

```
E W W H Y N O I T A G I R R I W A H S O E H
T G H O A G R I C U L T U R E E E G C R F C
E G A E R C A D Y F C R F P O D C N C C I T
K O E T R C E F A R E I A O G E N I O H L I
M L U S T H E R R L E S N E R F W D U A D D
C A A T S O M R L E T S R A E C O L N R L R
U D C W B H C I A U E O R R G T R O T D I A
L K O H O U K D R C W R T U S R U H R A W I
T C C U I D I E E E S I A E N F O A Y G K N
I H S A E N W L L I L I V N U B Y E S R C A
V E R E T E E B D I T R L R G M K L I O O G
A E W E A S A R Z I A C R A R E C B D N T E
T A U T S T Y E Y H N O S A G E I A E O S F
E H H E E H R A W A W G F S H E P R E M E R
N E P G K R O F H C T I P G R A N A R Y V U
R E E C D N A L M R A F F A R M H A N D I I
K V E H U S B A N D R Y C O M P O S T D L T
```

___ ___ ___

_____ ____?

_____ __ ___

___-_____!

ACREAGE FARMLAND LIVESTOCK VEGETABLE
AGRICULTURE FARMYARD MACHINERY WEATHER
AGRONOMY FERTILIZER NURSERY WEED KILLER
ARABLE FREE-RANGE ORCHARD WILDLIFE
COMPOST FRUIT ORGANIC
COUNTRYSIDE FURROW OUTBUILDING
COWSHED GRANARY PASTURE
CROFT HARVEST PICK YOUR OWN
CULTIVATE HAYSTACK PITCHFORK
DITCH HEDGEROW SCARECROW
DRAINAGE HOLDING SILAGE
FARMHAND HUSBANDRY THRESH
FARMHOUSE IRRIGATION TIED COTTAGE

102
Under the Sea

Can you find all these sea creatures in the grid?

BASS DACE HERRING
BREAM DORY MACKEREL
CARP FLOUNDER PERCH
COD GUPPY PIKE
CRAB HALIBUT PIRANHA
PLAICE
ROACH
SALMON
SARDINE
TUNA

D	H	A	L	I	B	U	T	F	D
P	O	T	L	F	P	M	T	A	S
E	I	C	E	L	L	A	C	B	S
N	Y	K	R	O	A	E	A	S	T
I	R	G	E	U	I	R	A	G	P
D	O	U	K	N	C	B	N	I	R
R	D	P	C	D	E	I	R	E	O
A	T	P	A	E	R	A	G	S	A
S	U	Y	M	R	N	P	R	A	C
O	N	T	E	H	P	E	R	C	H
E	A	H	A	N	O	M	L	A	S

Hey Presto!

Can you find all of these magic words in the grid?

ABRACADABRA
ASSISTANT
CAPE
CARD
CLOAK
CONJURER
DOVE
HEY PRESTO
HOCUS-POCUS
HOOP
LEVITATION
MAGIC CIRCLE
MAGICIAN
MATCHSTICKS
MYSTERY
PRESTIDIGITATOR
PROP
RABBIT
SAW LADY IN HALF
SHOWMANSHIP
SKILL
SLEIGHT OF HAND
TOP HAT
TRICKERY
VANISHING ACT
WAND

```
D T C D P N              H P T Y K P
  O I J W O X          G R O R A O
  V B A I E Z      V O P E O O
  E B T L S      P H T L H
    U A C A T A S C I
    T R W T Y L A
  M I I L M O E G A
  X V C A K A I N V
  E C D R S G I
B F W M O L I Y S S H H R T N N J
R O T A T I G I D I T S E R P E K
  G S W A N D S O I R I
  I E K M H C T F N U C
  C R Y I A Q A H A J K
  I P E P L L N A V N E
  A Y E D F L T N O O R
  N E U H R F L D C C Y
  S H O W M A N S H I P
  A R B A D A C A R B A
  H O C U S P O C U S P
  M A T C H S T I C K S
```

104
Soccer...

See if you can find all of these soccer words in the top grid.

BOOTS	PASS
DEFENSE	PENALTY
DRIBBLE	PITCH
FREE KICK	PLAYER
GOAL	REFEREE
HEADER	SOCCER
KICKOFF	STRIKER
LINESMAN	TACKLE
MATCH	THROWIN

```
R E D A E H F G W O
P L A Y E R F S G E
N F M H O G O A L T
E P R D C C K K A H
I E N E C T C S S R
M N R E E A I O T O
E A R E T K K P O W
L L T L F A I D O I
B T I C N E E C B N
B Y S O H F R A K P
I L I N E S M A N A
R T Y N D L G M I S
D N S R E K I R T S
A E S O T I L H A N
```

105
...Cleats

Now see if you can find all of these footwear items in the lower grid.

BALLET SHOES	MULES
CLOGS	PLATFORMS
FLIPFLOPS	SLIPPERS
GALOSHES	SNEAKERS
GUMBOOTS	TENNIS SHOES
HIGH HEELS	TRAINERS
LOAFERS	WELLIES
MOCCASINS	

```
K F L I P F L O P S
W E L L I E S W S S
G A L O S H E S R N
C U O B N I O T E E
C S A A R G H A P A
S M F L G H S N P K
R R E L U H S T I E
E O R E M E I A L R
N F S T B E N B S S
I T R S O L N U I S
A A N H O S E A G T
R L C O T R T O I N
T P A E S E L U M T
S N I S A C C O M R
```

106
Go Bananas!

One of these fruits can be found three times in the grid— but which one?

```
V G H C A E P T U A L S B S M C C
L D R S A T S U M A O L N U U L I
Y R R E B K C A L B A G I L L E T
Y E H K E E I K N C T O R T P M R
R R M U L N U W K K I O A A A E U
R O R P B M G C I Y U S D N G N S
E X P E Q A U A R S R E N A I T Y
B A J U B R R R G A F B A O F I A
P C A H R R E B P E N E M Q M N W
S T R A W B E R R Y O R B E A E C
A R N I E Z I D E R I R E N L K L
R T A U P C G M L F S Y A T I O B
W P L E O K I W I E S B U W A Z N
G B I T P L N E C T A R I N E D E
E N I R E G N A T Y P Y R R E H C
```

APPLE	CLEMENTINE	LEMON	PLUM
APRICOT	DATE	LIME	RASPBERRY
BANANA	ELDERBERRY	MANDARIN	RHUBARB
BLACKBERRY	FIG	MELON	SATSUMA
BLACKCURRANT	GOOSEBERRY	NECTARINE	STRAWBERRY
BLUEBERRY	GREENGAGE	PASSION FRUIT	SULTANA
CHERRY	KIWI	PEACH	TANGERINE
CITRUS	KUMQUAT	PEAR	

The fruit that can be found three times in the grid is _____ !

107
Bedtime

Can you find all of the listed bedtime words in the grid? When you have found them all, write out the leftover letters from top to bottom in the spaces below the grid to spell out a joke. This time, we've given you its punchline.

```
H O T E F D C U S H I O N Y W D O Y O U
E K R C E N A O R L W D R A O B D A E H
S R U N A E W E S E E O T H E N E B N D
A E N A T S I G T O T E M E O N B L I E
C T D L H E N D T S D S P I S S A A G B
W S L A E I A E E D D P O I L E F N H H
O L E V R Y L M Y R E E A P N P O K T G
L O I P B R I B N G D L B J R G S E C I
L B S E E T E H A M M O C K A U B T A E
I I D V D A N I K C U T W K E M O A P L
P A O E R M A T T R E S S N L O A F G S
G C B B E D S P R E A D T E N I S S A B
```

BASSINET	CUSHION	MATTRESS	SPRINGS
BEDSPREAD	DAY BED	NIGHTCAP	TEDDY BEAR
BEDSTEAD	EIDERDOWN	PILLOWCASE	TRUNDLE
BEDTIME STORY	FEATHER BED	PAJAMAS	TUCK IN
BLANKET	FOUR-POSTER	SLEEPING BAG	VALANCE
BOLSTER	HAMMOCK	SLEIGH BED	
COVERLET	HEADBOARD	SOFA BED	

___ ___ __ ____ ____

__ _____ __ _____

____ _ __ ____? WHEN YOU HEAR THEM SAWING!

Burger...

Tuck into this whopper of a puzzle. Find all of the listed words in the top grid.

BURGER	ORDER
COLD DRINK	PAPER BAG
COUNTER	PORTION
DRESSING	RELISH
FILLING	SALAD
FRIES	SHOP
LETTUCE	SNACK
LINE	SPICES
MEAT	TOMATO

```
H S C M A T A B H U N
O N O A T S A L A D G
S A U R E D R O E L A
E C N E C U T T E L B
C K T M R A N E A O R
I D E T M E F F F I E
P S R O E I L R L N P
S H T E L R I I O H A
U O A L S E E I S N P
S P I T S S T G E H O
C N E D A R I R R T I
G A N B O E E N L U G
N M I P S K M O G R B
C O L D D R I N K T I
```

```
F N L C O O K E D G R
Q R N L S N L N U O D
D E I R F P I H A E A
L G C T N M S S L P A
I N R O T A T I L T H
E A O U M E O I R A N
S T Q B O B R A S C F
T L U G A M I H D H R
N A E A P K B S E I I
D O T T S R E R M P E
E I T L O H U D A S S
B A E W N S E O E C R
U T N W E D G E R I J
C J A E L G D E C I D
```

...and Fries

Can you find all of these ways of serving potatoes in the bottom grid?

BAKED	FRIED
BOILED	FRIES
CHIPS	FRITTER
COOKED	HASH BROWN
CREAMED	MASH
CRISPS	ROAST
CROQUETTE	SAUTE
CUBED	WEDGE
DICED	

110
Word Search Race

Can you find all these watery words? You need a brother, a sister, or friend for this puzzle. One of you has the words on the right; the other takes the words on the left. Take turns searching for one of your words. There is a thirty-second time limit for each turn (the other person must time their opponent while they search). The first person to find all their words is the winner! Remember: no peeking at the grid while the other person takes their turn.

Words (left)	Grid	Words (right)
AQUEOUS	S R S U S W E R H D H I A U	SLOSH
BLOTCH	O Q T H A L E T I M M S P Y	SOAK
DABBLE	H Z U L O T O U A M S K A F	SOGGY
DAMP	S S L E T W Q P E R Q G L W	SOPPING
DIP	I O E A L I E R L N U U P X	SPECKLE
DOUSE	W P L D L C S R B D I T M R	SPLASH
DRENCH	S P Z E D E H T B D R E A Q	SPLATTER
DRIZZLE	S I Z G O Z B Y A F T I D S	SPRAY
FLUID	Y G I G S O A K D Y N N U R	SPRINKLE
FOAM	J Q R O E G R E M B U S M G	SPUME
IMMERSE	N A D L S P R I N K L E N S	SQUELCHY
LIQUID	S Y A R P S A K H S E I I L	SQUIRT
MIST	O P M E C F Q H X C P G V O	SUBMERGE
MOIST	G W L T O R U F O P T U C S	SWISH
PADDLE	G N S A E X E C O S W O M H	WADE
RUNNY	Y I M W S S O S P E C K L E	WALLOW
SATURATE	M O I S T H U P A D D L E B	WASH
SHOWER	H C N E R D S O W L F D J S	WATERLOGGED
SLOP	V P Z B L B A E D J A I S L	WET
	W Y E H U T T M Q W V P K D	

NFL - AFC

NFL stands for the National Football League, the largest and oldest professional football league in the United States. The NFL is made up of 32 teams, in two conferences, the American Football Conference (AFC) and the National Football Conference (NFC).

```
S X Y M U M P H Y U M F R H U P R Y E D R
F N S L A G N E B I T A N N I C N I C G M
E E H P I T T S B U R G H S T E E L E R S
I W E O U T R S R E D I A R D N A L K A O
H Y E P W O B A L T I M O R E R A V E N S
C O E D E N V E R B R O N C O S C D T R F
Y R E O G M H T S N A X E T N O T S U O H
T K U R E I Y E O C D A L R T P I E A O R
I J A C K S O N V I L L E J A G U A R S O
C E E S N W O R B D N A L E V E L C T H L
S T U I I N D I A N A P O L I S C O L T S
A S G M A E T E N N E S S E E T I T A N S
S S T O I R T A P D N A L G N E W E N C D
N B U F F A L O B I L L S K R T I A E F L
A R E O S N I H P L O D I M A I M P A W T
K I H Y U S R E G R A H C O G E I D N A S
```

BALTIMORE RAVENS

CINCINNATI BENGALS

CLEVELAND BROWNS

PITTSBURGH STEELERS

HOUSTON TEXANS

INDIANAPOLIS COLTS

JACKSONVILLE JAGUARS

TENNESSEE TITANS

BUFFALO BILLS

MIAMI DOLPHINS

NEW ENGLAND PATRIOTS

NEW YORK JETS

DENVER BRONCOS

KANSAS CITY CHIEFS

OAKLAND RAIDERS

SAN DIEGO CHARGERS

112
NFL - NFC

The team that wins the the AFC championship faces the winner of the NFC championship in the Super Bowl at the end of each season.
Let's see if you are an expert by finding all the teams on both pages.

```
O S N O C L A F A T N A L T A V Z U U S M
C P H I L A D E L P H I A E A G L E S R I
S M N E W Y O R K G I A N T S F U D M E N
I U S L A N I D R A C A N O Z I R A S H N
C D E E M F E D R H U T E P V R E O T T E
N T Y E D R U G M H E O T R E B I L L N S
A P O S Y O B W O C S A L L A D E D O A O
R T S K W A H A E S E L T T A E S R U P T
F F I E L C H I C A G O B E A R S O I A A
N W A S H I N G T O N R E D S K I N S N V
A G M H T U R E I Y E O D L R T E P R I I
S R E E N A C C U B Y A B A P M A T A L K
I B O R E T H U L I G M E C D V O R M O I
T I E N E W O R L E A N S S A I N T S R N
F L R E O P S N O I L T I O R T E D T A G
G R E E N B A Y P A C K E R S I H N Y C S
```

CHICAGO BEARS	DALLAS COWBOYS
DETROIT LIONS	NEW YORK GIANTS
GREEN BAY PACKERS	PHILADELPHIA EAGLES
MINNESOTA VIKINGS	WASHINGTON REDSKINS
ATLANTA FALCONS	ARIZONA CARDINALS
CAROLINA PANTHERS	SAN FRANCISCO
NEW ORLEANS SAINTS	SEATTLE SEAHAWKS
TAMPA BAY BUCCANEERS	ST. LOUIS RAMS

113
Floating

All of the words listed below can be found in the top grid. One is hidden TEN times in the grid, but the others appear only once. Can you find them all?

BOAT

CANOE

DINGHY

LI-LO

PEDALO

RAFT

RUBBER RING

SAILBOARD

```
C P R O P U W A B J P T E M
Z H L A G T F A R E F Z O K
Z I T M F N L X D A R E D V
L U F M H T I A R F S F L R
B O A T W H L R X R A F T T
D B R R T O E A R Y I Y K A
I I A J F P O F P E L S N O
D F N V A U N T A L B X S E
T B R G D A C F G O B Y J
I I F G H S C X B A A I U C
T F A R K Y R T T K R V W R
Q N O U G O G Q F Z D E Q N
```

114
Dancing

```
M S W I N G I K Z A L P J C
A O Q J A W L J U K B I F U
S N O S A A A I V R V M X D
L L L N W E C V F E Y Q U H
A A N N W B R E A K I N G R
S O O C A A G N I K A E R B
S O J E B B L J M G B P O X
M W E H M O B K T G B O A R
P O I S U O H C V Y G W L T
P A T N R G H P V I M Q T Y
W O Z G G I D P E K F D R S
M N T J U E A K X I S I Z R
```

Each of these words can be found twice in the grid. How quickly can you find all 16?

BOOGIE

BREAKING

JIVE

MOONWALK

RUMBA

SALSA

SWING

TAP

115
Beach Barbecue

Can you find all the barbecue words in the grid? Once you've solved the puzzle, write out the leftover letters from top to bottom in the spaces below the grid to spell out the punchline to the joke.

BBQ SAUCE
BEEF
BREAD ROLL
BUN
CHICKEN
CHIPS
COLESLAW
COOKED MEAT
CORN ON THE COB
DRUMSTICK
FRESH MEAT
GARLIC BREAD
GRILLED CORN
BAKED POTATO
KEBAB
KETCHUP
LAMB
MUSTARD
ONION
PITA BREAD
PORK CHOP
RELISH

SALAD
SAUSAGE
SPARERIB
STEAK

R	B	D	A	E	R	B	A	T	I	P	N	U	B
E	P	O	R	B	O	N	S	C	O	L	A	M	B
L	I	N	C	N	R	A	E	H	H	S	C	T	A
I	K	R	I	E	L	E	C	K	A	I	A	L	K
S	E	O	C	A	H	K	A	U	C	E	P	D	E
H	N	C	D	O	R	T	S	D	M	I	R	S	D
S	K	D	U	O	L	A	N	D	R	U	H	R	P
P	P	E	P	A	G	E	E	O	M	O	A	C	O
A	U	L	B	E	S	K	S	S	N	T	L	F	T
R	H	L	E	A	O	Q	T	L	S	R	E	L	A
E	C	I	D	C	B	I	B	U	A	E	O	O	T
R	T	R	C	N	C	I	M	B	B	W	O	C	O
I	E	G	N	K	T	A	E	M	H	S	E	R	F
B	K	S	G	A	R	L	I	C	B	R	E	A	D

What's a hedgehog's favorite food?

___ ___ ___ ___ ___ ___ ___ ___ ___ ___   ___ ___ ___ ___ ___ ___!

116
Serial Joker

Which do you prefer, playing pranks or being serious? Look for the words in the grid to find out.

CHUCKLE   LAUGH   TRICK
DETERMINED   READING   THOUGHTFUL
FOOL   PRANK
EARNEST   REALISTIC
FRIGHT   SHOCK
INTELLIGENT   SENSIBLE
JOKE   SURPRISE
PRACTICAL   SERIOUS
KIDDING   TRAP
RATIONAL   SINCERE

```
R D T S W R L Z J S G R L V D M L U H Z E Q
J S E E K A P A O X K S A U Y U G W L C B X
L H N N S U R P R I S E I T F T H G I R F G
D D A S I F H S K K P N W T I C I V G N N K
T R Q I O M L G I E T Y H F Z O O X N I C C
P A T B E K R D U E C G M P C U N J D S H O
H P M L G A D E L A U L A C I T C A R P U H
X Y F E D I R L T O L L R M T E E D L O C S
H Q A D N E I N H E H N J S R B L G K K Q
H I Y G X G R T E G D S W T I E Z O P Z L I
J T P S E R I O U S F W V L C R D Y G E I
O E R N F C B Y E O T J C B A N T R I C K P
K E T A K A O C O U T R B Q E I M A X J I V
E I V H P O I L M T Q F U U R S Z N K W B F
```

Snowman

The children are building a snowman. Help them by looking for the listed words in the grid. You will not be able to find one of the words—this is the snowman's name.

ANORAK
ARMS
BLANKET
BODY

BROOMSTICK
BUTTONS
CANE
CAP
CARDIGAN

CARROT
CLOAK
COAL
COAT
EARS
EYES
FEET
FINGERS
FROST
GLOVES
HAIR
HAT
HEAD
ICE
LADDER
LEGS
MOUTH
MUFF
NIPPY
NOSE
PEBBLES
PIPE
ROCKS
SCARF
SMILE
SNOWBALLS
TOES

118
Disney Heroes

Now it's the turn of the male Disney characters. See how quickly you can find them all.

ALADDIN
ARCHIMEDES
ARTHUR
BALOO
BAMBI
BASIL
BEAST
CAPTAIN HOOK
CHIP
DONALD DUCK

DUMBO
EDWARD
ELLIOT
ERIC
GEPPETTO
GOOFY
HERCULES
JAFAR
JOHN SMITH
KENAI

KUZCO
MICKEY MOUSE
MILO
MOWGLI
MUFASA
NEMO
PETER PAN
PINOCCHIO
PHILLIP
PHOEBUS

PLUTO
PRINCE CHARMING
PUMBAA
RAFIKI
SIMBA
SHANG
STITCH
TARZAN
TIGGER
TIMON

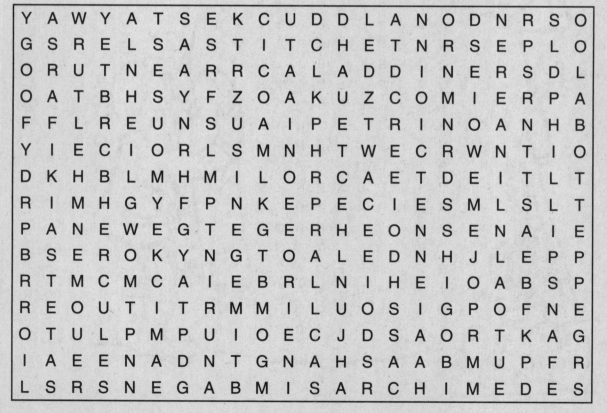

```
Y A W Y A T S E K C U D D L A N O D N R S O
G S R E L S A S T I T C H E T N R S E P L O
O R U T N E A R R C A L A D D I N E R S D L
O A T B H S Y F Z O A K U Z C O M I E R P A
F F L R E U N S U A I P E T R I N O A N H B
Y I E C I O R L S M N H T W E C R W N T I O
D K H B L M H M I L O R C A E T D E I T L T
R I M H G Y F P N K E P E C I E S M L S L T
P A N E W E G T E G E R H E O N S E N A I E
B S E R O K Y N G T O A L E D N H J L E P P
R T M C M C A I E B R L N I H E I O A B S P
R E O U T I T R M M I L U O S I G P O F N E
O T U L P M P U I O E C J D S A O R T K A G
I A E E N A D N T G N A H S A A B M U P F R
L S R S N E G A B M I S A R C H I M E D E S
```

119
Pathfinder

This puzzle is similar to a word search. Can you find a path through this grid that includes all the types of boats? You can move up, down, or sideways, but not diagonally. We've found the first one, SAMPAN, for you!

CATAMARAN
CORACLE
CRUISER
CUTTER
DHOW
DORY
DRIFTER
FELUCCA
FERRY
GONDOLA
JUNK
KETCH
LIFEBOAT

G	E	R	R	R	B	O	A	C	A	T	D	R
G	U	N	A	O	W	S	T	C	S	H	C	I
T	L	T	A	C	E	L	L	U	H	I	A	F
N	M	A	A	C	L	O	E	F	T	P	Y	T
U	A	R	R	H	C	O	P	O	A	I	L	E
P	N	A	O	C	T	I	L	B	E	F	R	R
S	A	E	R	G	E	N	C	U	T	T	E	D
P	M	M	A	O	K	E	R	R	A	U	S	O
A	N	T	E	N	E	C	A	I	M	B	Y	R
U	J	S	E	D	A	D	N	N	E	F	U	I
N	D	D	L	O	L	H	N	I	R	E	R	S
K	A	P	E	U	R	O	W	P	R	Y	C	E
P	I	R	O	G	E	N	O	O	H	C	S	R

LINER
LUGGER
NARROWBOAT
PADDLE STEAMER
PINNACE
PIROGUE
PUNT

SAMPAN
SCHOONER
SHIP
SLOOP
SUBMARINE
YACHT

120
Extreme Weather

This a word search about the weather. Do you like wrapping yourself up before going out, or do you think that just a light jacket is enough to protect you from the wintry weather? Let's see how quickly you find all the words.

```
Q F Q B F W B S H H G N Y F K E Q C J
L R B I V L T V O Z A N N F Z A I R P
K O Y Y H E A Q T S L S I B R T E D Q
I Z L N A C W M G V Z W H Z C O P L P
S E K M S E A R I N G E O R E R S G B
G N I H C R O C S N G L A U T E I T R
W N X Y G T S Y G E G T S O T I R E Y
G A R T N D R M N E B E R Z M H T F J
X I R A I J W K I D O R S U L T R Y C
M A P M T M A D L G I I O J I O V R O
N Y L L I H C O I D V N X B T X F E W
D P T C B D C F O Z A G C O O L W I E
K M Y U J E L R B U K C N C F U L F H
```

ARCTIC	FLAMING	SULTRY
BITING	FREEZING	SWELTERING
BITTER	FROSTY	TORRID
BLEAK	FROZEN	WARM
BOILING	HOT	
CHILLY	ICY	
COLD	SCORCHING	
COOL	SEARING	
FIERY	STEAMING	

Sports Stuff

Can you find the listed sports equipment in the grid? When you've found them all, write the leftover letters from top to bottom in the spaces below to spell out a joke and its punchline.

BAILS	GLOVES	SHIRT	STRINGS
BATON	GOGGLES	SHOES	STRIP
BLOCKS	GRIP	SHORTS	STUDS
BOOTS	HELMET	SHUTTLECOCK	STUMPS
BOWLS	HURDLE	SKIS	SURFBOARD
CADDY	JAVELIN	SNOWBOARD	TABLE
CLUBS	PADS	SOCKS	TRACKSUIT
COSTUME	POLE	SPIKES	TRAINERS
DISCUS	RACKET	STICK	TRUNKS

```
E P W E S H R A S K N U R T T S I K S T
M T I T L A D S H C A D D Y S E C O Y R
U O U R C B G U U S E R G K R L M T V I
T D E K G N A B T U T A C L U J R L N H
S R E N I A R T T S N O W B O A R D E S
O T H R G O G G L E S B S O C V S T U H
C E T U S A B T E K D F A K E E E C S B
A S T E R T A N C I A R S T O L S S T O
B O O T S D I N O P P U I H O I O S R W
S P M U T S L C C S I S S B D N A P I L
S K C O L B S E K T S H O R T S L L P S
```

___ ___ __ ___ _____

___ ___ ____?

_ _____ ____!

122
Spring

The listed spring flowers can be found in the word search. One of the words is hidden TEN times in the grid, but the others appear only once. Can you find them all?

BLUEBELL
CROCUS
DAFFODIL
HYACINTH
IRIS
PRIMROSE
SNOWDROP
TULIP

E	F	J	S	S	I	I	D	C	Q	B	J	L	T
J	F	I	W	I	S	R	S	I	R	H	Q	U	D
L	R	O	H	R	Z	I	L	K	L	O	L	M	S
I	L	R	D	I	C	S	R	I	F	I	C	T	P
N	P	E	I	R	I	S	D	I	P	I	N	U	W
A	O	Y	B	E	S	O	R	M	I	R	P	G	S
K	R	B	A	E	F	H	Y	A	C	I	N	T	H
M	D	Z	W	F	U	Z	I	K	Y	S	R	I	U
R	W	I	A	T	S	L	E	P	P	G	R	I	O
T	O	D	D	R	I	X	B	E	X	I	C	X	S
V	N	S	S	I	R	I	Q	L	S	C	L	O	V
N	S	B	K	V	I	X	U	Y	A	G	H	M	U

123
Summer

Listed below there are 8 words related to summer, and they can each be found twice in the bottom grid. Can you find all 16 words?

CRABS
PEBBLES
ROCK POOLS
SAND
SEAWEED
SHELLS
STARFISH
WAVES

S	B	Y	J	F	L	H	S	X	S	D	S	O	S
E	W	A	V	E	S	E	S	L	W	E	N	A	Z
L	K	C	L	K	A	X	O	I	V	C	N	A	J
B	R	T	R	W	V	O	D	A	F	D	C	U	S
B	U	O	E	A	P	F	W	V	X	R	R	T	L
E	Q	E	C	K	B	H	S	I	F	R	A	T	S
P	D	C	C	K	W	S	D	S	B	S	B	T	H
O	G	O	T	D	P	M	S	H	S	L	S	W	S
M	R	E	Z	O	A	O	N	E	Y	L	G	A	G
S	E	A	W	E	E	D	O	L	R	E	E	H	Q
S	E	L	B	B	E	P	P	L	N	H	R	E	P
N	I	S	Q	U	Z	K	I	S	S	S	P	B	C

124
Fall

Each of these trees that lose their leaves in the fall can be found three times in the grid below. How quickly can you find all 24 words?

ASH
BEECH
CHESTNUT
HAZEL
HOLLY
HORNBEAM
OAK
SYCAMORE

A	R	F	X	S	H	C	C	S	L	Y	M	S	H
S	W	I	I	C	B	H	N	Y	W	L	A	Z	T
H	C	E	E	B	E	E	S	C	O	L	E	S	T
G	O	E	K	S	O	S	K	A	O	O	B	U	H
E	B	R	T	A	L	T	K	M	U	H	N	E	Q
U	H	N	N	Y	O	N	Y	O	B	T	R	R	G
R	U	C	L	B	Q	U	V	R	S	Z	O	O	C
T	P	L	E	F	E	T	H	E	A	T	H	M	H
E	O	X	L	E	Z	A	H	A	C	H	A	A	Y
H	O	L	L	Y	B	C	M	J	Z	K	Z	C	K
H	O	R	N	B	E	A	M	M	N	E	V	Y	P
S	Y	C	A	M	O	R	E	D	L	D	L	S	M

125
Winter

G	Z	I	L	L	S	S	F	T	L	S	L	M	Z
R	N	I	G	I	N	E	F	O	E	I	E	R	F
A	A	I	W	G	O	L	C	L	G	C	G	O	F
H	J	N	N	H	W	A	A	H	I	K	G	T	Q
L	I	A	H	T	S	G	T	G	A	L	E	S	B
D	H	W	N	N	H	N	Y	K	O	C	M	E	U
G	V	I	O	I	I	G	N	S	S	F	X	C	A
L	A	W	H	N	G	N	I	N	T	H	G	I	L
R	I	L	G	G	S	E	A	L	O	O	W	S	H
P	A	A	E	S	T	O	R	M	R	J	R	A	I
S	X	I	H	S	R	A	I	N	M	Y	I	M	C
M	W	O	N	S	B	T	V	P	O	L	I	C	E

All these winter words can be found four times in the puzzle. Can you find all 32 words?

FOG
GALES
HAIL
ICE
LIGHTNING
RAIN
SNOW
STORM

126
On the Up-and-Up

This word search is based on climbing.
Can you find all the hidden words?

I	U	G	K	W	I	S	N	I	N	I	N
T	U	I	G	N	M	A	S	T	C	D	I
L	N	S	E	T	U	F	I	E	N	S	T
C	E	T	U	O	R	E	P	A	C	S	E
Y	A	P	F	O	O	T	H	O	L	D	D
G	Y	R	P	E	C	Y	D	R	G	L	M
N	R	A	A	A	I	H	N	E	O	H	A
A	O	S	L	B	R	A	T	H	E	R	S
H	C	F	I	E	I	R	D	L	E	E	L
R	K	U	A	R	B	N	M	N	V	L	S
E	E	C	O	D	A	E	E	O	R	L	T
V	I	P	A	H	T	S	M	R	B	A	E
O	E	B	O	O	T	S	L	G	N	W	M

BELAY
BOOTS
CARABINER
ESCAPE ROUTE
FOOTHOLD
HELMET
HANDHOLD

MOVES
OVERHANG
ROCK
RAPPEL
ROPE
SAFETY HARNESS
WALL

127
Earth, Wind, and Fire

Hidden in the first grid there are five words related to EARTH, in the second grid
there are five words related to WIND, and in the third grid there are five words
that can come after FIRE. Can you find them all?

EARTH

W	O	R	L	D	M	X
D	E	O	T	L	A	A
T	E	B	E	P	N	Q
K	Z	K	N	G	I	H
C	R	Z	A	N	B	F
S	O	I	L	U	M	J
U	S	W	P	Y	Q	V

WIND

T	K	C	D	J	B	Y
L	T	R	R	L	R	U
B	I	S	A	E	E	M
A	A	S	U	F	E	Q
V	T	X	G	G	Z	P
S	G	R	H	H	E	I
K	D	N	T	O	W	Z

FIRE

M	D	E	S	B	R	M
V	R	P	I	R	E	L
Q	I	A	C	I	T	G
P	L	C	L	G	H	N
Z	L	S	J	A	G	E
R	U	E	T	D	I	H
O	X	B	Y	E	F	K

128
Up, Up, and Away

Can you find all of these ballooning words in the grid? We've put one in to help get you started. One of the words in the list can be found three times in the grid. Can you spot which one it is?

ADVENTURE
ALOFT
ASCEND
BALLOON
BASKET
BURNER
CAPSULE
COCKPIT
COLORFUL
DESCEND
DRIFT
EXCITING
FLAME
~~FLIGHT~~
FLOAT
GLIDE
GONDOLA
HEIGHT
HOT AIR
INFLATE
LAND
LAUNCH
LIFT
PANORAMA
PILOT
SCENERY

SKY
SOAR
SUSPENDED
TAKEOFF
TREAT
TREETOPS
VIEW
WICKER

```
            C O C K P I T X M
          Y M S B M S D W H E Y S
        T I P K C O C S R L L R T N R
      S G M T A E R T U U I I B A E N R
      H H E I G H T S S L U F R O L O C
    D V I E W F U N P P I E T T L V T G B
    N N R E L E O A R E N R U B F I A N A
    T S E I R O C A I N F L A T E Y K I S
    E R G C L U R G N D P W R S S M E T K
    I H E L S S T G D E I A I O K P O I E
    T H A E I A L N N D L E A C A Y F C T
      B O U T I R N E E O R T N K T F X
      A B E D O S W C V T O O E F E R E
      Y E M A P N S I D R H O E H R
      R G A S S E O A A L G C C
      E O L M D M D A H N O
      N N F A U N A U C
      E D R E A A K
      C O N L P I
      S L I S
      E T A
```

129
Word Search Race

To solve the puzzle, you need a brother, a sister, or a friend. One of you
has the words on the left and one has the words on the right. Take turns
searching for one of your words—but there is a thirty-second time limit
for each turn (the other person must time their opponent while they
search). The first person to find all their words is the winner! Remember:
no peeking at the grid while the other person takes their turn.

SABLE	SALT
SABOTAGE	SALUTE
SABER	SALVAGE
SACHET	SALVO
SACK	SAME
SACRED	SAMPLE
SACRIFICE	SANCTION
SADDLE	SANDAL
SAFARI	SANE
SAFE	SAPPHIRE
SAFFRON	SARCASM
SAIL	SARDINE
SAINT	SASH
SAKE	SATCHEL
SALAD	SATELLITE
SALARY	SATISFY
SALE	SATURATE
SALIENT	SAUNA
SALIVA	SAUSAGE
SALLOW	SAVAGE
SALMON	SAWDUST
SALON	SAY

```
E S G T P H E M N V T X Y U
S A C H E T T O S N R R D I
V T S A S H I W E A A I E J
F I N K X T L I O L C Q R Y
O S C I C L L S A L A R C C
S F A N A A E S A N L T A N
A Y A L S S T S U D W A S S
L S J L O M A A E S D A S S
E F A S W N S P H G C L A R
S A B O T A G E P R K L E Q
L E H C T A S S I H U O E S
W O F N A Y A F A T I L B A
G M B O F C I X E Y P R D L
E I T M K C S Q C M E S E A
S M L L E E A S A N A S S D
E A A A N L T S A L V A G E
Z G K S I B U S V F U F R A
K J A E D A R O D S F A E S
N P S V R S A S A I L R P Z
A V I L A S T G Y Z U I O L
E R B A S S E S A N D A L N
```

130
Snowball Fight

It's pretty good fun when you have a snowball fight. Join in the fun and look for all the words listed below in the snowflake.

BALLS
BEE
BLIZZARD
COLD
DRIFT
DRIP
ENJOY
FALL
FIGHT
FLAKES
FREEZE
FUN
GUST
HIT
ICICLE
JOLLY
LAUGH
MOUSE
MUTT
PAWS
PLAY
RAIN
SIMON
SKATE

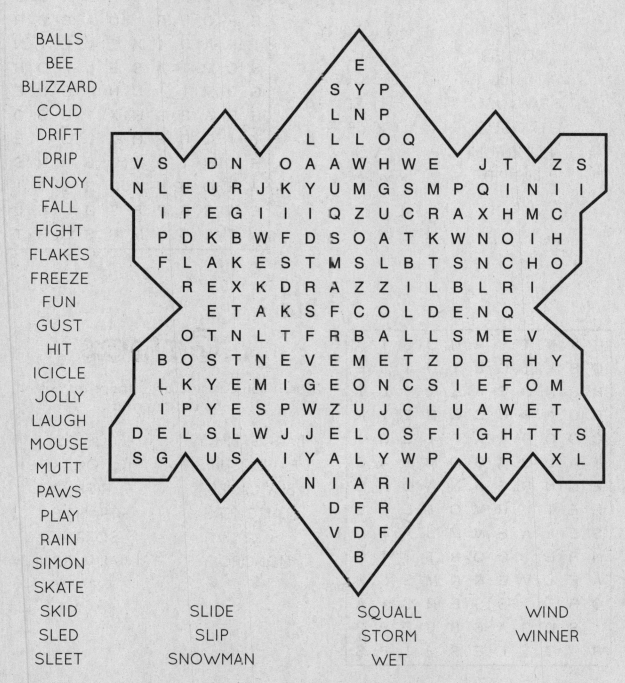

SKID	SLIDE	SQUALL	WIND
SLED	SLIP	STORM	WINNER
SLEET	SNOWMAN	WET	

Bored...

Yawn! Can you work up enough enthusiasm to find all of these boring words?

APATHY	MONOTONY
BOTHER	PALL
DULL	TEDIOUS
EXHAUST	TIRED
FATIGUE	TROUBLE
HUMDRUM	VEX
INSIPID	WEARY

```
Y N O T O N O M G F T
W V A P A T H Y N I S
N D S R A E M G R T N
S E I R A U I E N E S
E F O P R L D A B D R
I E A D I X E V E I N
S O M T A S E L L O R
G U M I I N N E B U E
H B A P S G X I U S O
Y T O R F H U L O I E
R L H T A A L E R N S
A E O U H A D R T T I
E A S B P E E D U L L
W T L G N M R S O R T
```

...Games

See if you can find all of these games in the bottom grid.

BACKGAMMON	PARCHEESI
BATTLESHIPS	PICTIONARY
BUCCANEER	RISK
CHECKERS	SCRABBLE
CHESS	SORRY
MONOPOLY	TRIVIAL PURSUIT

```
G V N T Y R R O S T K
C B L I G B Y N T S E
H U N U E A L O I L T
E C A S U C O R E Y N
C C O R A K P T E R I
K A L U G G O M I A S
E N N P E A N A O N E
R E T L R M O I E O E
S E L A H M M U A I H
N R E I O O R T I T C
A E L V G N N M S C R
O R T I S S E H C I A
I S C R A B B L E P P
B A T T L E S H I P S
```

133
A Good Book

One of these book-related words can be found three times in the grid.
Can you spot which one it is?

```
M O E S T O R Y F N E N D I N G E
R P T K J Q M M S F O N O S N M G
E U O C I P E S K I W I C V F H A
A S U S E N T E N C E H T I E N S
D B Q E V I T A R R A N C I Y L S
E C E T W R E L D R L T S I D E A
R E A S O R A G A N I S Y I U E P
P L U H T N I C A O T M G G F B C
E A T G R S T T N P E D O N H A A
S U R U O E E K E I R L L V U E U
A T O A R L O L N R A D O T I S T
S J O Y B O I R L I T R H C D O H
L G N L B L M P D E U O T I S R O
A C H A P T E R E K R W N H N P R
Y R A R B I L E A B E I A M A R D
```

ANTHOLOGY	EDITION	NARRATIVE	QUOTE
AUTHOR	ENDING	NOVEL	READER
BESTSELLER	EPIC	OPUS	SENTENCE
BOOK	EPILOGUE	PAGE	STORY
CHAPTER	FICTION	PARABLE	TALE
CHARACTER	JOURNAL	PASSAGE	WORD
DIALOGUE	LIBRARY	PLOT	WRITER
DRAMA	LITERATURE	PROSE	

The word that can be found three times in the grid is _____ !

Dog...

Can you find all of these dog names in the top grid?

BENJI	GOLDIE	REX
BOBBY	JASPER	ROVER
BONNIE	LASSIE	RUSTY
BOUNCER	LUCKY	SCAMP
BULLSEYE	MUFFIN	SCRUFFY
BUSTER	PATCHES	SNOWY
BUTCH	PICKLE	SPARKY
FIDO	POPPY	

```
R E V O R J G M B W P
V E X B D A A U T A O
H I X U A Y T S T G P
M N E L Y C K C P I P
T N I L H K H R J E Y
D O D S A E C N A I R
N B L E S N E U T P A
H I O Y N B I Y L Y S
A T G E E L F F B T S
F I D O A F S B F S C
R E T S U B O N D U A
L R S R G B M I O R M
P I C K L E N E A W P
E S B O U N C E R O Y
```

...and Bone

See if you can find all of these bones in the bottom grid.

```
Y E W J M S U I D A R
M L X O O U R U M E F
A K V D S T I R R U P
N C O E H A H N E N S
D U C O R U N N A T E
I N D A M T O V I R T
B K R E R B E N I A C
L V R E W P S B R L A
E U E A M A A S R O L
S T J T L M A L H A U
I I E U N L A S O T P
Y B B E D I N H E S A
O I A L L E T A P T C
F A F I C O C C Y X S
```

ANVIL	KNUCKLE
CARPAL	MANDIBLE
COCCYX	PATELLA
CRANIUM	RADIUS
FEMUR	SCAPULA
FIBULA	STIRRUP
HAMMER	TARSAL
HUMERUS	TIBIA
JAWBONE	VERTEBRA

136
From A to Z

One of these words can be found three times in the grid—but which one?

```
F W L E V V J Z L X E C U D O R P
Q E E A L C A A N A S R F E A N D
S C D Y C G T L E M O N R N R I N
A O O N T I G R U B M I S O K H E
R L Y I G S E U I E D A N H P O K
R O E I A H A R N D W A H P N B E
O G D L T C T T L S T C O O S B E
L Y R A D H T E A U I N U L B Y W
O G F A D D R R R S T I T Y T B G
C M L A F A I A E U E C S X N R Y
H S Y I I O L M P S E N I M S A J
Q U E S T I O N K T S E D P V A L
N R E I S T I N O A T E E C L R G
N M I S A K E H E O T U M P I R E
T S E Z R E N R Y B B B O H E A I L
```

ACTRESS	HOBBY	OUTSIDE	VALUE
BIRTHDAY	INPUT	PRODUCE	WEEKEND
COLOR	JASMINE	QUESTION	XYLOPHONE
DIGITAL	KNEE	RIDDLE	YODEL
ECOLOGY	LEMON	SNUGGLE	ZEST
FATHER	MIDDLE	TASTY	
GLITTER	NATURAL	UMPIRE	

The word that can be found three times in the grid is _____ !

137
Going Away

Find all the different types of luggage in the grid. Then write the leftover letters in the spaces below to spell out the punchline to the joke!

BRIEFCASE
CAMERA CASE
CARPETBAG
CARRIER
CARRYALL
CONTAINER
DUFFEL BAG
FLIGHT BAG
GLADSTONE BAG
LAUNDRY BAG
OVERNIGHTER
PURSE
RUCKSACK
SADDLEBAG
SCHOOL BAG
SHOPPING BAG
SHOULDER BAG
VALISE
VANITY CASE
WALLET

```
K C A S K C U R G B O G
G W O E R P C A A V V A
A A U N U E B S E E A B
B L B R T T I R T G N G
L L S E E A N R A L I N
O E A P N I I B R L T I
O T R U G O E N H A Y P
H A E H N L T Y E Y C P
C F T O D D R S G R A O
S E O D T T R H D R S H
R V A L I S E Y E A E S
E S A C F E I R B C L I
S H O U L D E R B A G G
G A B L E F F U D R G T
G A B T H G I L F R U N
C A M E R A C A S E K S
```

Why couldn't the elephants go swimming?

_ _ _ _ _ _ _ _   _ _ _ _   _ _ _ _ _ _   _ _ _ _ _

_ _ _ _ _ _ !

Picnic...

See if you can find all of these picnic-related words in the top grid.

ANT	GRASS	SPOON
BASKET	HAMPER	THERMOS
BLANKET	INSECT	TREAT
COOL BOX	NAPKIN	TUMBLER
CUTLERY	RUG	VIEW

```
Y W V C X I I H I L G
W E I V U E C A I N R
S E O L A T R H T U E
I N S E C T L U I E P
N N S O T A M E Y E M
X C I N L B R B R G A
M O A K L I T L N Y H
E A B E P E P A S T O
R I R L K A E N L A H
U A N S O G N K S E E
O C A R R O T E I R A
R B E A L G C T N T M
S U S S O M R E H T O
R S G S P O O N T I A
```

...Basket

Now see if you can find all of these basketball words in the lower grid.

```
D H I G H G S Y K V J
A L M N A B P S D M N
A U R O O I H C A O C
I O A U V L R E G P S
N F N O E E T D R A H
I C T N Y E M T S L O
E A R A I N R E S A T
T Y L E C U D E N L R
J P G I O N E A F T S
T U S C O R E R L E F
T I M E O U T I I K R
E L H P A N S E N S O
C D R T I A E L E A G
E L B B I R D N S B M
```

BASKET	HIGH	PLAYER
BOUNCE	JUMP	REFEREE
COACH	LINES	SCORE
COURT	MOVEMENT	SHOT
DRIBBLE	PASS	TEAM
FOUL	PIVOT	TIME-OUT

140
Cheesy Does It!

See if you can find all these types of cheese in the grid. There's also another cheese that's not in the list hiding somewhere in the grid—can you spot it?

```
F T K E L A D Y E L S N E W B V E S R O M R
O R E D L E I C E S T E R L P R S A D Q K E
N O V R L A T N E M M E I O K I I G L P F T
T F T O E M A D E A A M H M W R O E O E B S
I U R Q N Y I T T N B S O S E U I D W U L E
N A E U I Y U T T U I Z C T D C P E S L U C
A E B E N M O R R B Z O S A E I Y R T B E U
P B M F T C A G G A R E N S R L I B O H C O
R N E O I G E N R N H O T A L P F Y C S H L
O O M R S R I E C C K E S I D E O E V I E G
V T A T T K L B L H R C H D M A B N T N E E
O L C I N L O I O S E P H N N U P Y E A S L
L I F I A U S S H P R G A E W I O A B D E B
O T T T R I M I N E Y S O G D B W L N A A U
N S I S B A R P A R M E S A N D T D L A B O
E R I H S E H C E R I H S A C N A L E A R D
N N G O R G O N Z O L A D M A T U R E R H G
```

The cheese that is hiding in the grid is

_____ !

BABYBEL   ESROM   MATURE
BEAUFORT   FETA   MOZZARELLA
BLUE CHEESE   FONTINA   PARMESAN
BOURSIN   GORGONZOLA   PROVOLONE
BRIE   GOUDA   RED LEICESTER
CAERPHILLY   GRANA PADANO   RED WINDSOR
CAMEMBERT   GRUYERE   RICOTTA
CHESHIRE   HALLOUMI   ROQUEFORT
COTSWOLD   ILCHESTER   SAGE DERBY
DANBO   LANCASHIRE   SAMSO
DANISH BLUE   LEICESTERSHIRE   STILTON
DOUBLE GLOUCESTER   LIMBURGER   STINKING BISHOP
EDAM   MANCHEGO   SWISS
EMMENTAL   MASCARPONE   WENSLEYDALE

141
Ice Cream Flavors

Each of these words can be found twice in the grid. How quickly can you find all 14?

CHOCOLATE
PISTACHIO
RASPBERRY
STRACCIATELLA
STRAWBERRY
TUTTI FRUTTI
VANILLA

R	A	S	P	B	E	R	R	Y	G	Y	Q	B	C
D	C	T	C	H	O	C	O	L	A	T	E	S	A
O	K	Z	U	Y	R	R	E	B	W	A	R	T	S
M	P	I	S	T	A	C	H	I	O	F	P	R	K
U	A	L	L	E	T	A	I	C	C	A	R	T	S
S	T	R	A	C	C	I	A	T	E	L	L	A	A
V	A	N	I	L	L	A	F	G	H	L	X	L	L
N	Y	R	R	E	B	W	A	R	T	S	B	Y	L
E	T	A	L	O	C	O	H	C	U	X	W	T	I
Y	R	R	E	B	P	S	A	R	A	T	Q	I	N
T	U	T	T	I	F	R	U	T	T	I	T	E	A
O	I	H	C	A	T	S	I	P	E	V	J	I	V

142
Leaf It to Me!

Look for all of the listed trees in the grid. Be careful, though, one of the trees in the list cannot be found in the grid.

ASH
BEECH
DOUGLAS FIR
ELM
HORSE CHESTNUT
LARCH
MAPLE

MONKEY PUZZLE
OAK
POPLAR
REDWOOD

SCOTS PINE
SEQUOIA
SILVER BIRCH
SPRUCE
SYCAMORE
WALNUT
~~WILLOW~~
YEW

143
Just Desserts!

Find all of these desserts in the grid.

```
W H E F R U I T C R U M B L E A A
T A I T I C E C R E A M S S P P S
A B P C H A T S F B A H S C E P V
L A Y P O G U L L R E U U I T L S
E N R S L T I E E R O S E R I E E
M O R U P E M L R M T U A U T C L
A F E N M H S Y E A O T D A S H O
R F H D C B T T R D T N P E F A R
A E C A D R A D R I L I T T O R E
C E E E I L S B U U O E I A U L T
E P N F O L G R A C D M G G R O I
M I L C I I F C A E C E R N S T F
E E O C E G N A M C N A L B A T O
R H E T R A T L L E W E K A B E R
C E A P E A C H C O B B L E R M P
```

ANGEL DELIGHT	CREME CARAMEL	PEACH MELBA
APPLE CHARLOTTE	CUSTARD SLICE	PETITS FOURS
APPLE STRUDEL	FRUIT CRUMBLE	PROFITEROLES
BAKEWELL TART	FRUIT TART	RUM BABA
BANOFFEE PIE	GATEAU	SHERRY TRIFLE
BLANCMANGE	ICE CREAM	SUNDAE
CHERRY PIE	LEMON TART	TAPIOCA
CHOCOLATE MOUSSE	PEACH COBBLER	

```
G N I K L A W S H S B
Y N J R X O W T A S G
A L I A U I O E H E N
R E A G M N S P E N I
L M R M G P N P O T P
T E I O U O K I G I P
R N E H B E J N N F I
G A S S E I I G E G K
O U S P I N C L A S S
P L F T I C A S B R I
H I E A O A R T Y E T
T C R L R M E E A O U
T T R O W I N G X R P
F E G N I L C Y C E S
```

Fit...

See if you can find all of these fitness words in the top grid.

AEROBICS	RUNNING
CYCLING	SIT-UPS
EXERCISE	SKIPPING
FITNESS	SPIN CLASS
JOGGING	STEPPING
KEEP FIT	SWIMMING
PUSH-UPS	TRAINING
ROWING	WALKING

```
A L O I V I O L I N H
F N R E T T I C N A Q
V I O L O N E E R Y L
E L D D I F S P H G N
S O T A C I Z Z I P I
S O B R M E C H S G L
T T I A E E B Y C U O
A N S G L M R E K I D
M I Z L N A I U R T N
B U O I T A L C D A A
O Q G I T E R A L R M
U E S N L H E A I U P
R R S E F E E H S K D
A P S A L T E R Y N A
```

...as a Fiddle

Can you find all of these stringed instruments in the bottom grid?

BALALAIKA	MANDOLIN	TAMBOURA
CELLO	PIZZICATO	UKULELE
CITTERN	PSALTERY	VIOLA
DULCIMER	REBEC	VIOLIN
FIDDLE	REQUINTO	VIOLONE
GUITAR	SAMISEN	ZITHER
HARP	SARANGI	
LYRE	SITAR	

146
Jumbo Puzzle

Can you find all of these elephant-related words in the grid?

```
S Z T N A H P E L E K N U R T W X N
K B H U H E R B I V O R E L M R A L
S D L A M M A M H I N U N A B I L N
U P E Z B U E O T R A C O D S N L A
T F O T E I W A T E T R I A S K E C
S O L P C D T H F S I X T O N L C I
N R B E A E I A C E O Y A D H E I R
A E A H G C T S T R N Y V E U D T F
I S O E K G H O T V A M R A E P N A
D T V S E U R Y R E L D E O E L A C
N E K I G G S A D P P O S M V H G A
I I T E Y E R C S E A D N L O I I L
N S A V A N N A H S R W O R I R G F
G N I V O M W O L S K M C G R A Y S
```

AFRICAN	HABITAT	MAMMAL	SLOW MOVING
ASIAN	HEAVY	MEMORY	THICK SKIN
CALF	HERBIVORE	NATIONAL PARK	TRUNK
CONSERVATION	HERD	PACHYDERM	TUSKS
ELEPHANT	HOWDAH	PROTECTED	VEGETATION
FOREST	HUGE	RESERVE	WRINKLED
GIGANTIC	INDIAN	ROAM	ZOO
GRASS	IVORY	SAVANNAH	
GRAY	LARGE EARS	SIX TON	

Along Came a Spider

See if you can find all of these spider-related words in the grid.

```
J R O O D P A R T F A N G S X Y S G
W E A S E B P L N C D A E R H T Y O
N O E L A S W R A E C I A E T S E L
A P D T U A O T E A D B I L E E S D
M H H I R T C U S D D R I O F T X E
S O O C W H N D M O A S A D F F A N
T B E R F K I A M O G T R G U U R O
N I P L B N C E R E N A O V M N O R
U A I L H W N A L A I E R R S N H B
H E L C E I E T L N T S Y O S E T T
S Y A U E C H A L B R E I S I L S K
K R E O C G U T V R N E T P M W I L
A L P S I K C A B E L D D I F E O I
M O N E V E Y C T R R N I N B B E S
B I R D E A T I N G S J U M P I N G
```

ABDOMEN
ARACHNID
BATH
BIRD-EATING
BITE
BLACK WIDOW
CATCH FLIES
CRAWL
DRAIN

EIGHT LEGS
FANGS
FIDDLEBACK
FUNNEL WEB
GARDEN
GOLDEN ORB
HUNTSMAN
JUMPING
LUCKY

MISS MUFFET
MONEY
ORB WEAVER
PHOBIA
PREDATOR
SAC
SILK
SPIN
TARANTULA

THORAX
THREAD
TRAPDOOR
VENOM

148
Time to Go

It's been fun, but all good things must come to an end.
Help this guy find everything he needs to pack to go home.
The leftover letters will spell out the punchline to the joke.

BICYCLE
BOOKS
CAMERA
CARDS
FLEECE
HAMMOCK
LAUNDRY BAG
MAGAZINE
PAJAMAS
ROPES
SAUCEPAN
SHAMPOO
SHOES
SHORTS
SLEEPING BAG
SNEAKERS
SOCKS
SUNGLASSES
SUNTAN LOTION
SWIMSUIT

TOOTHBRUSH
TOOTHPASTE

TROUSERS

```
S O O P M A H S E S K C O S
B U A E T O O T H B R U S H
G O N S N Y S O I E W G E P
A E O T N I R E L T A O U A
B S T K A T Z C P B T K S J
Y A I S S N Y A G O S C T A
R U S D A C L N G W R O R M
D C E N I P I O I A S M O A
N E C B E P H M T H M M U S
U P E E E A S T O I A A S N
A A E E D U K E O T O H E H
L N L E I R S E E O I N R T
W S F T C A M E R A T A S S
S E S S A L G N U S D R A C
```

How did you find the weather at camp?

_ _ _ _ _ , _ _ _ _ _ _ _ _ _ _ _

_ _ _ _ _ _ _ _ _ _ _ _ _ _ _ _ !

Solutions

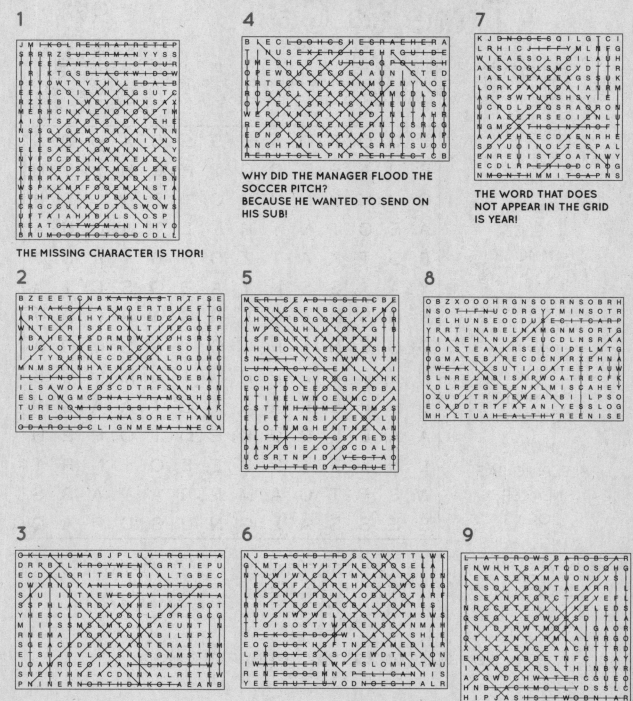

1

THE MISSING CHARACTER IS THOR!

2

3

4

WHY DID THE MANAGER FLOOD THE
SOCCER PITCH?
BECAUSE HE WANTED TO SEND ON
HIS SUB!

5

6

7

THE WORD THAT DOES
NOT APPEAR IN THE GRID
IS YEAR!

8

9

WHAT DO SEA MONSTERS EAT?
FISH AND SHIPS!

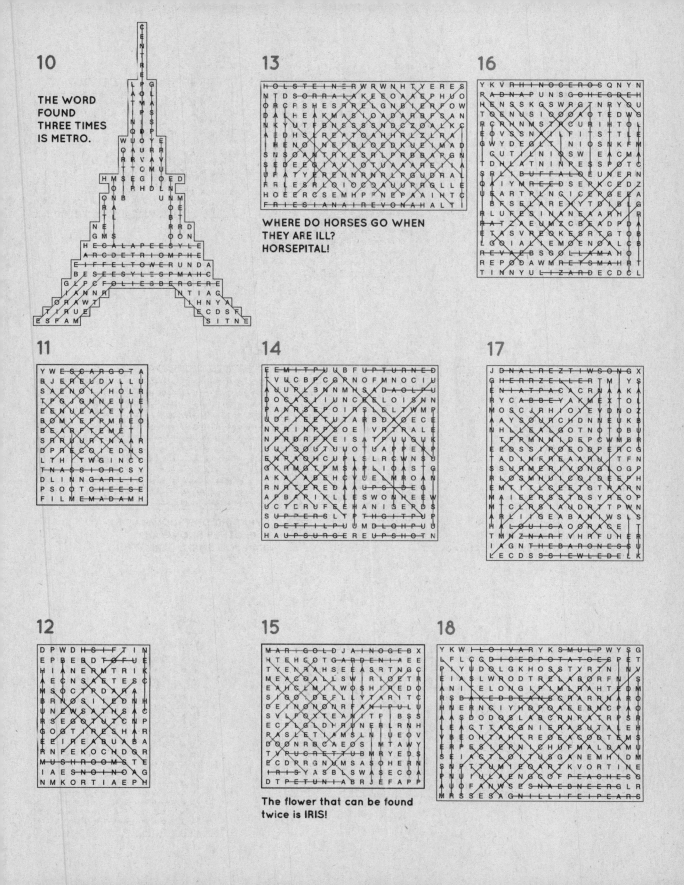

10

THE WORD FOUND THREE TIMES IS METRO.

13

WHERE DO HORSES GO WHEN THEY ARE ILL? HORSEPITAL!

16

11

14

17

12

15

The flower that can be found twice is IRIS!

18

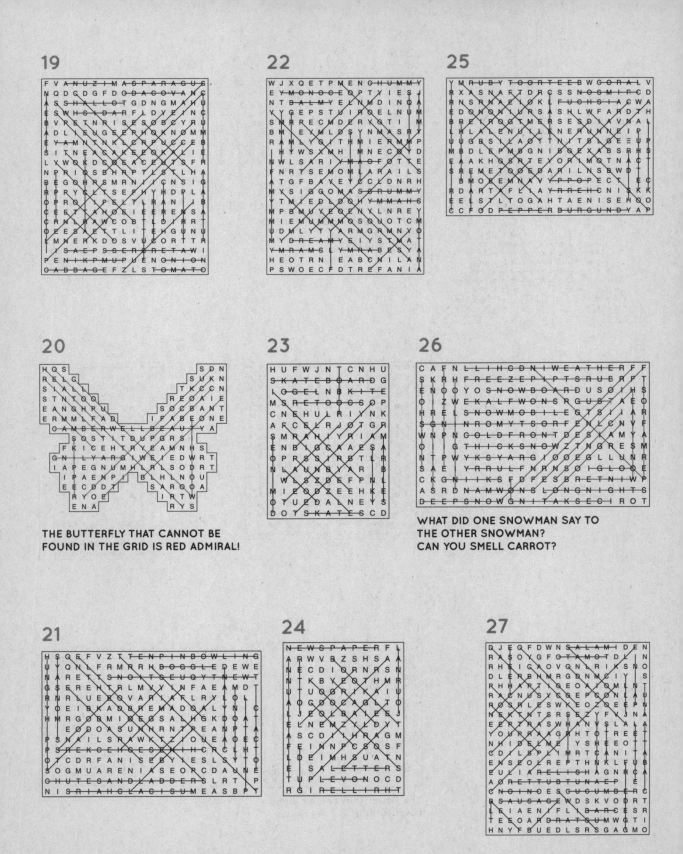

19

22

25

20

THE BUTTERFLY THAT CANNOT BE
FOUND IN THE GRID IS RED ADMIRAL!

23

26

WHAT DID ONE SNOWMAN SAY TO
THE OTHER SNOWMAN?
CAN YOU SMELL CARROT?

21

24

27

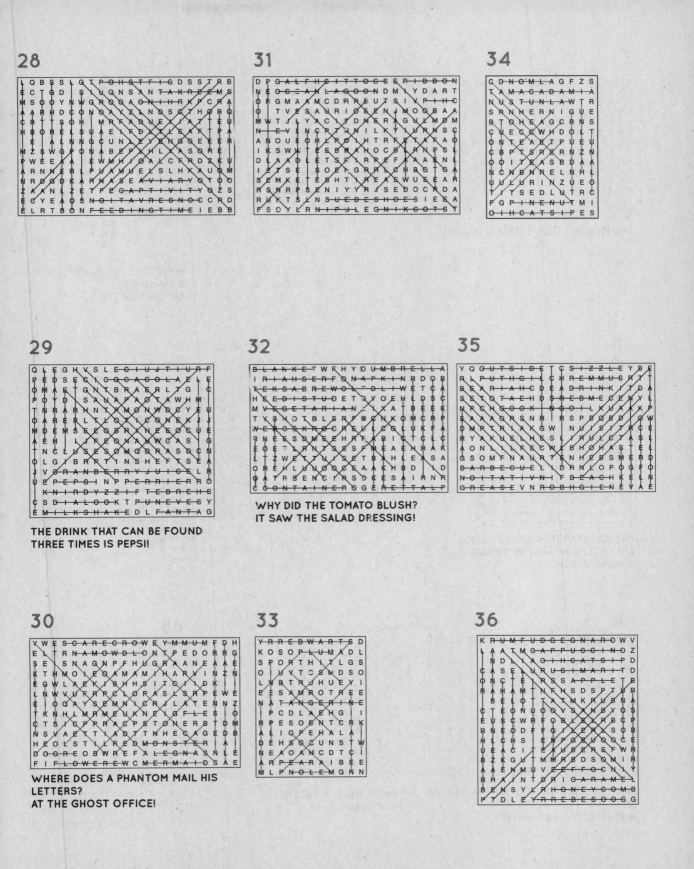

28

29

THE DRINK THAT CAN BE FOUND
THREE TIMES IS PEPSI!

30

WHERE DOES A PHANTOM MAIL HIS
LETTERS?
AT THE GHOST OFFICE!

31

32

WHY DID THE TOMATO BLUSH?
IT SAW THE SALAD DRESSING!

33

34

35

36

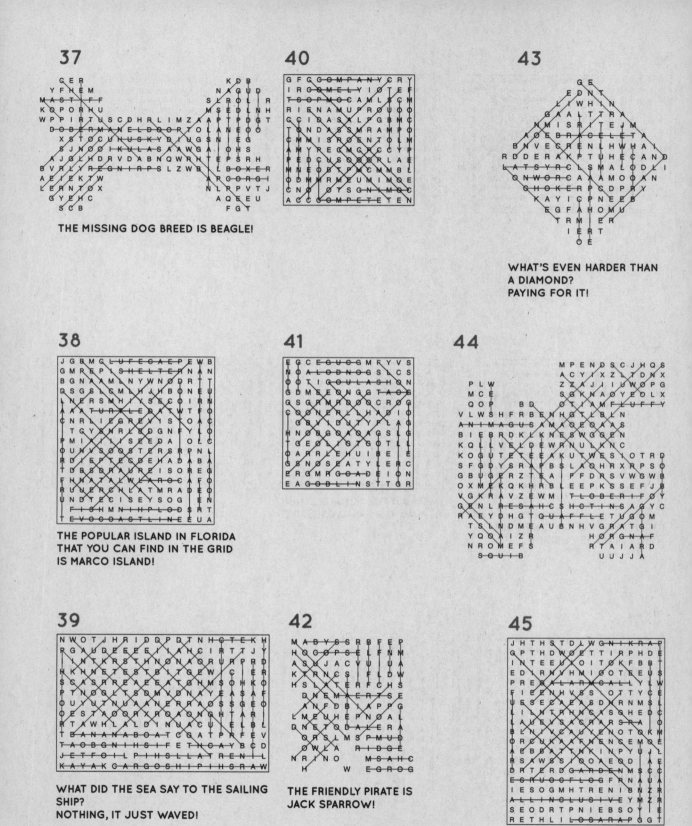

37

THE MISSING DOG BREED IS BEAGLE!

40

43

WHAT'S EVEN HARDER THAN A DIAMOND?
PAYING FOR IT!

38

THE POPULAR ISLAND IN FLORIDA THAT YOU CAN FIND IN THE GRID IS MARCO ISLAND!

41

44

39

WHAT DID THE SEA SAY TO THE SAILING SHIP?
NOTHING, IT JUST WAVED!

42

THE FRIENDLY PIRATE IS JACK SPARROW!

45

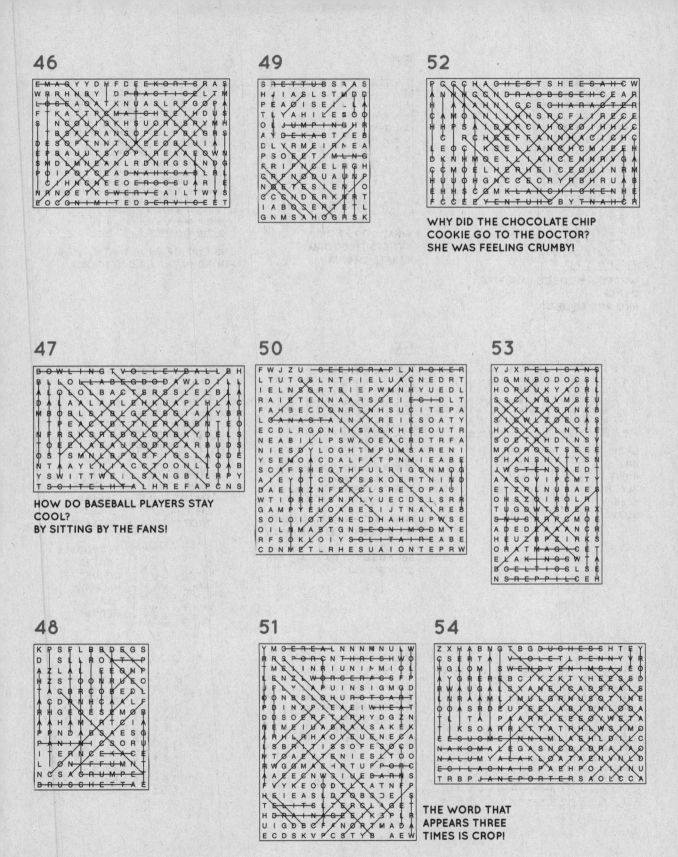

46

49

52

WHY DID THE CHOCOLATE CHIP
COOKIE GO TO THE DOCTOR?
SHE WAS FEELING CRUMBY!

47

50

53

HOW DO BASEBALL PLAYERS STAY
COOL?
BY SITTING BY THE FANS!

48

51

54

THE WORD THAT
APPEARS THREE
TIMES IS CROP!

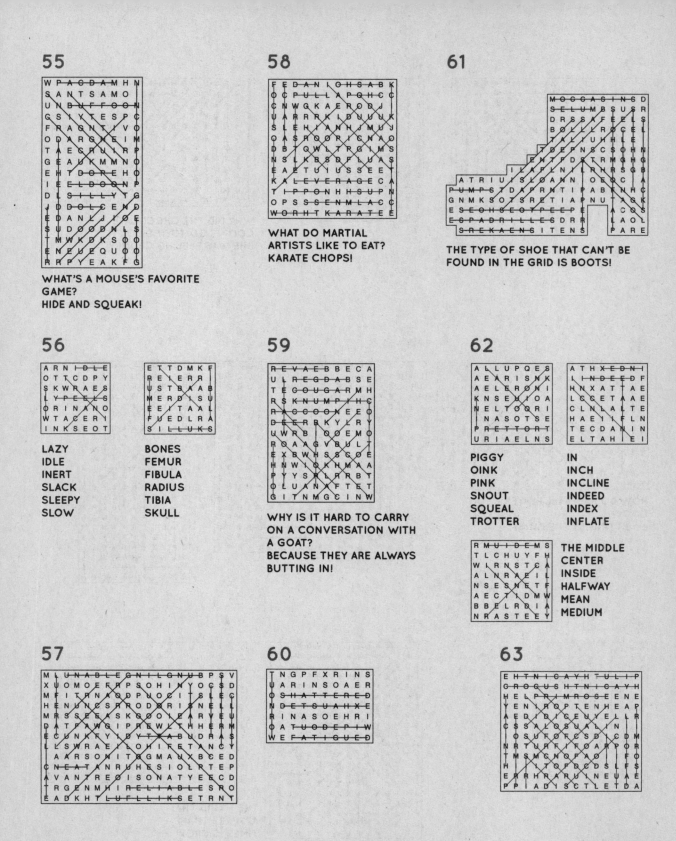

55

WHAT'S A MOUSE'S FAVORITE
GAME?
HIDE AND SQUEAK!

58

WHAT DO MARTIAL
ARTISTS LIKE TO EAT?
KARATE CHOPS!

61

THE TYPE OF SHOE THAT CAN'T BE
FOUND IN THE GRID IS BOOTS!

56

LAZY
IDLE
INERT
SLACK
SLEEPY
SLOW

BONES
FEMUR
FIBULA
RADIUS
TIBIA
SKULL

59

WHY IS IT HARD TO CARRY
ON A CONVERSATION WITH
A GOAT?
BECAUSE THEY ARE ALWAYS
BUTTING IN!

62

PIGGY
OINK
PINK
SNOUT
SQUEAL
TROTTER

IN
INCH
INCLINE
INDEED
INDEX
INFLATE

THE MIDDLE
CENTER
INSIDE
HALFWAY
MEAN
MEDIUM

57

60

63

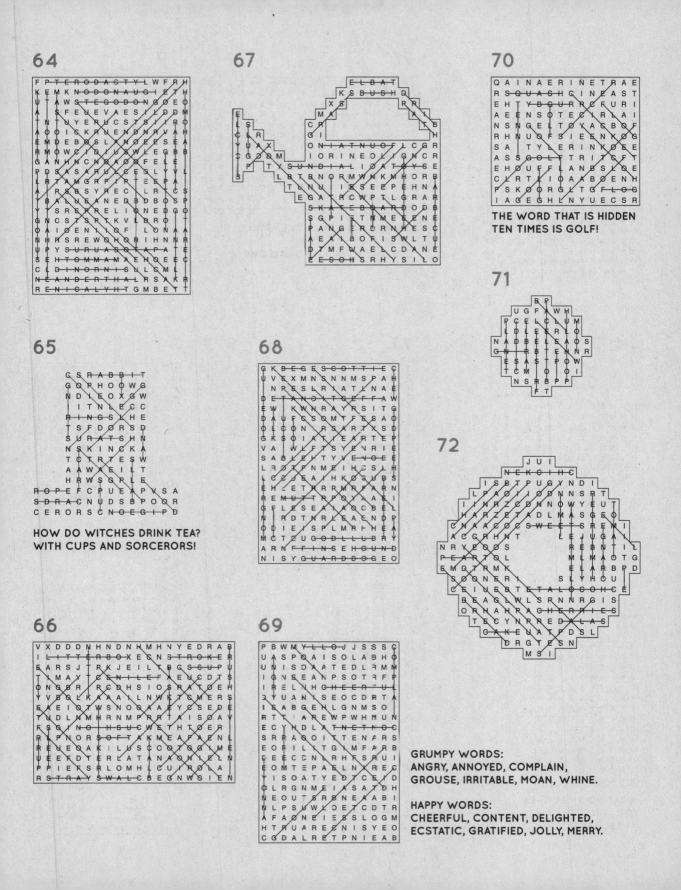

64

67

70

THE WORD THAT IS HIDDEN
TEN TIMES IS GOLF!

71

65

68

HOW DO WITCHES DRINK TEA?
WITH CUPS AND SORCERORS!

72

66

69

GRUMPY WORDS:
ANGRY, ANNOYED, COMPLAIN,
GROUSE, IRRITABLE, MOAN, WHINE.

HAPPY WORDS:
CHEERFUL, CONTENT, DELIGHTED,
ECSTATIC, GRATIFIED, JOLLY, MERRY.

73

76

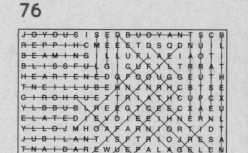

DID YOU HEAR THE JOKE ABOUT THE
HUGE EASTER EGG?
IT'S QUITE HARD TO SWALLOW!

79

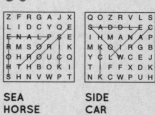

74

77

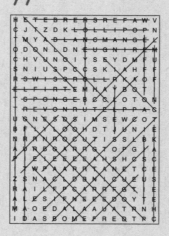

80

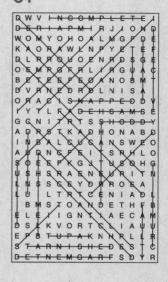

SEA   SIDE
HORSE   CAR
PLANE   KICK
PORT   LINE
SHORE   SADDLE
SICK   SHOW

75

WHAT DO THIEVES EAT
FOR LUNCH?
HAMBURGLARS!

78

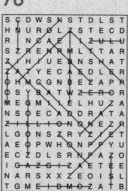

81

82

THE WORD THAT DOES NOT APPEAR IN THE GRID IS WITCH!

85

88

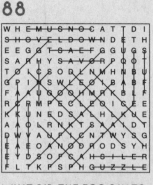

WHAT DID THE EGG SAY TO HIS FRIEND? HEARD ANY GOOD YOLKS!

83

86

89

84

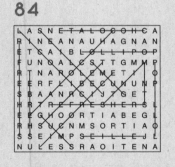

87

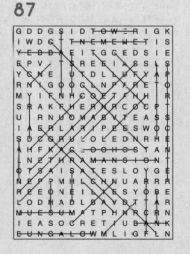

90

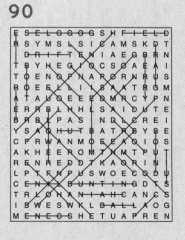

91

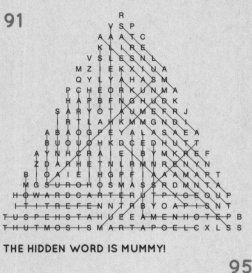

THE HIDDEN WORD IS MUMMY!

94

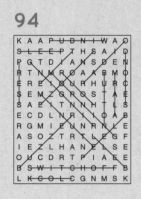

97

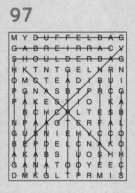

92

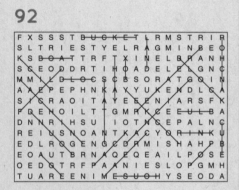

95

THE FIVE SNAKES THAT CAN
BE FOUND TWICE IN THE GRID
ARE ADDER, COBRA, PYTHON,
RATTLESNAKE, AND VIPER!

98

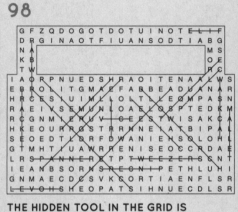

THE HIDDEN TOOL IN THE GRID IS
HACKSAW!

93

96

99

100

```
C K W V E N N S C R N S O U
R G N S E L H E F T Y O T P
C R A H N S B O T A R H U E
N S T O D A T A E C R A G M
I I N E A E P S T O T R D R
L F I E H U L A N R S D E E
O C D R T I A I B E Q L D G
N M N I M B L E C S K P A O
R M T I A E P W H A N U O E
C A D L S R A O I T T E L N
A S R S E O I L T Y G E M F
Y G M I L F A B T E C D P N
R H S U B I H O T E O P V
A V L N U R G E I S N O A T
E E C L D I L R G O N M I S
A K K H E E O U E T R E N E
A Y B W I L A R P S W L O E
C D T R F A O I N I E S L
O G M H T U U A R R E G N I
Y S E O S C D A L Y R A T P
```

LIGHT HEAVY
AIRY BULKY
AGILE HARD
DELICATE HEFTY
FLIMSY LOADED
LITHE MASSIVE
NIMBLE PONDEROUS
PORTABLE WEIGHTY

101

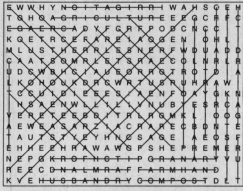

WHY WAS THE COCKEREL SAD?
BECAUSE HE WAS HEN PECKED!

102

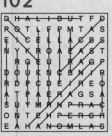

103

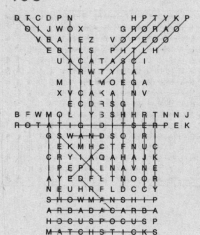

104

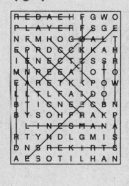

105

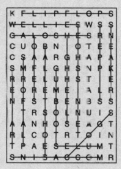

106

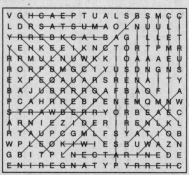

THE FRUIT THAT CAN BE FOUND
THREE TIMES IN THE GRID IS KIWI!

107

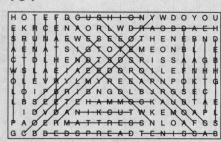

HOW DO YOU KNOW WHEN
SOMEONE IS SLEEPING LIKE A LOG?
WHEN YOU HEAR THEM SAWING!

108

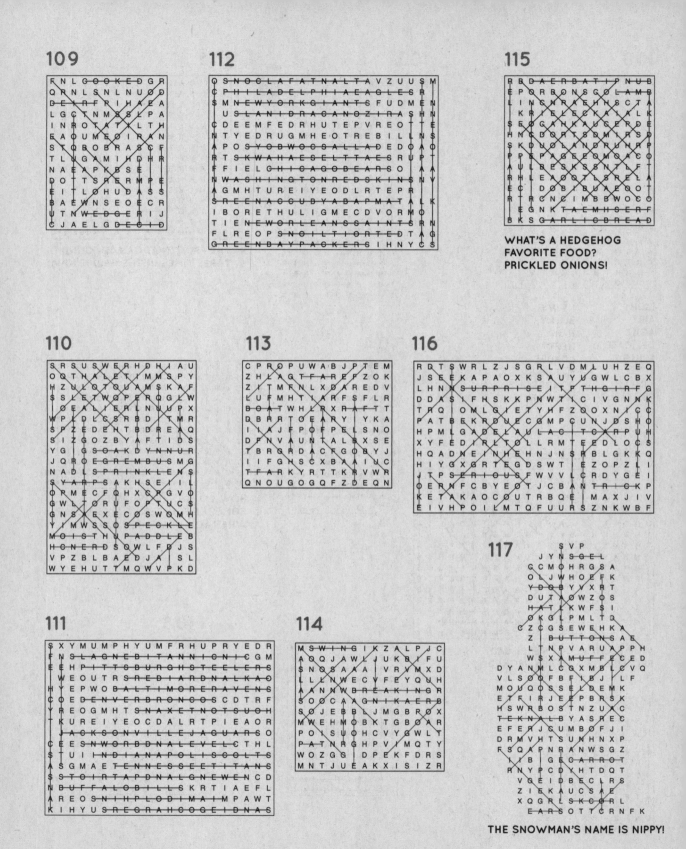

109

110

111

112

113

114

115

WHAT'S A HEDGEHOG
FAVORITE FOOD?
PRICKLED ONIONS!

116

117

THE SNOWMAN'S NAME IS NIPPY!

118

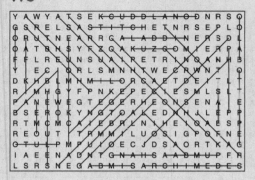

```
Y A W Y A T S E K C U D D L A N O D N R S Q
G S R E L S A S T I T C H E T N R S E P L O
O R U T N E A R R G A L A D D I N E R S D L
O A T B H S Y F Z G A K U Z G O M I E R P A
F F L R E U N S U A R E T R I N O A N H B
Y E C O R L S M N H T W E C R W N T Q
D K H B L M H M I L O R G A E T D E I L T
R M H G Y F P N K E P E E I E S M L S L
P A N E W E G T E G E R H E O N S E N A E
B S E R O K Y N G T O A K E D H J L E P P
R T M C M C A I E B R N I H E I O A E S P
R E O U T T R M M I L U O S I G P O F N E
O T U L P M P U I O E C J D S A O R T K A G
I A E E N A D N T G N A H S A A B M U P F R
L S R S N E G A B M I S A R C H I M E D E S
```

119

THE TYPES OF BOATS ARE FOUND IN THIS ORDER: SAMPAN, JUNK, PIROGUE, PADDLE STEAMER, GONDOLA, DHOW, PINNACE, KETCH, CORACLE, CATAMARAN, PUNT, LUGGER, NARROWBOAT, SLOOP, LINER, CUTTER, LIFEBOAT, FELUCCA, SHIP, YACTH, DRIFTER, DORY, SUBMARINE, FERRY, CRUISER, SCHOONER.

120

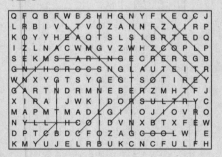

```
Q F Q B F W B S H H G N Y F K E Q C J
L R B I V L T V O Z A N N F Z A R P
K O Y Y H E A Q T S L S I B R T E D Q
I Z L N A C W M G V Z W H Z C O P L P
S E K M S E A R I N G E C R E R S G B
G N I H C R O C S N G L A U T E I T R
W N X Y G T S Y G E G T S O T I R E Y
G A R T N D R M N E B E R Z M H T F J
X I R A J W K D O R S U L T R Y C
M A P M T M A D L G I O J I O V R O
N Y L L H C O D V N X B T X F E W
D P T C B D C F O Z A G G O O L W I E
K M Y U J E L R B U K C N C F U L F H
```

121

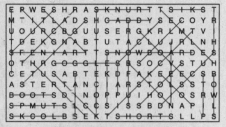

```
E R W E S H R A S K N U R T T S I K S T
M T I T L A D S H G A D D Y S E C O Y R
U O U R C B G U U S E R G R L M T V
T B E K G N A B T U T A C L U J R L N H
S F E N J A R T T S N O W B O A R D E S
O T H R G O G G L E S B S O C Y S T U H
C E T U S A B T E K D F A K E E E C S B
A S T E R T A N C A R S T O L S S T O
B O O T S D N O P P U I H Q O S R W
S P M U T S L C C S I S S B D N A P L
S K O O L B S E K T S H O R T S L L P S
```

WHAT DO YOU SERVE BUT NOT EAT? A TENNIS BALL!

122

```
E F J S S I D G Q B J L T
J F I W S R S I R H Q U D
L R O H R Z L K L O L M S
I E R D C S R I F C T P
N F E I R I S D I P N U W
A C Y B E S O R M I R P G S
K R B A E F H Y A C N T H
M D Z W F U Z I K Y S R I U
R W I A T S L E P P G R I O
T O D D R X B E X I C X S
V N S S I R I Q S C L O V
N S B K V X U A G H M U
```

123

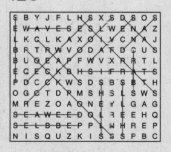

```
S B Y J F L H S X S D S O S
E W A V E S E S L W E N A Z
L K C L K A X O I V C N A J
B R T R W V O D A F D C U S
B U G E A P F W V X R R T L
E C E C K B H S I F R T S
P D C C K W S D S B S B T H
O G O T D R M S H B L S W S
M R E Z O A O N E Y L G A G
S E A W E E D O L R E E H Q
S E L B E E P D L W H R E P
N I S Q U Z K I S S S P B C
```

124

```
A R F X S H C C S L Y M S H
S W I I C B H N Y W L A Z T
H C E E B E E S C O L E S T
G O E K S O S K O O B U H
E B R T A L T K M U H N E Q
U H N N Y O N Y O B T R R G
R U C L B Q U V R S Z O O C
T P L E F E T H E A T H M H
E O X L E Z A H A C H A A Y
H O L L Y B C M J Z K Z C K
H O R N B E A M M N E V Y P
S Y C A M O R E D L D L S M
```

125

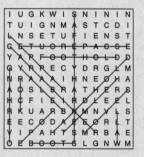

```
G Z I L L S S F T L S L M Z
R N I G N E F O E I E R F
A A I W G O L C L G C G O F
H J N N H W A X H K G T Q
L I A H T S G T G A L E S B
D H W N N H N Y K Q C M E U
G V I O I G N S S F X C A
L X W H R G N X H G H
R I L G G S E A L O Q W S H
P A A E S T O R M R J R A
S X I H S R A I N M Y I M C
M W O N S B T V P O L I C E
```

126

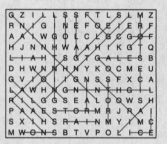

```
I U G K W I S N I N I N
T U I G N M A S T C D I
L N S E T U F I E N S T
G E T U O R E P A O S E
Y A R F O O T H O L D
G X R R E C Y D R G L M
N R A A I H N E O H A
A O S L B R A T H E R S
H C F I E I R D L E E L
R K U A R B M N N L S
E E C O D A E B O R L T
V I P A H T S M R B A E
O E B O O T S L G N W M
```

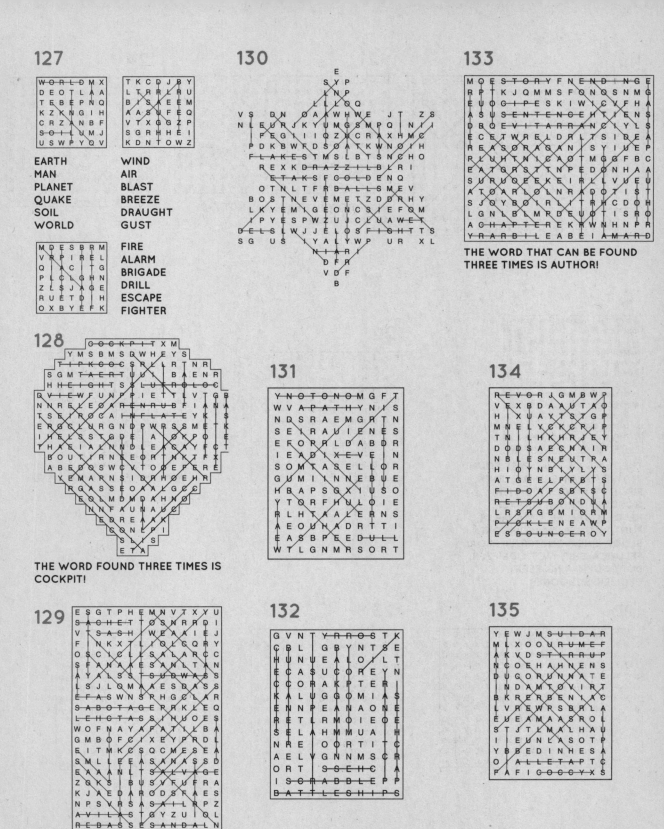

127

EARTH
MAN
PLANET
QUAKE
SOIL
WORLD

WIND
AIR
BLAST
BREEZE
DRAUGHT
GUST

FIRE
ALARM
BRIGADE
DRILL
ESCAPE
FIGHTER

130

133

THE WORD THAT CAN BE FOUND
THREE TIMES IS AUTHOR!

128

THE WORD FOUND THREE TIMES IS
COCKPIT!

131

134

129

132

135

136

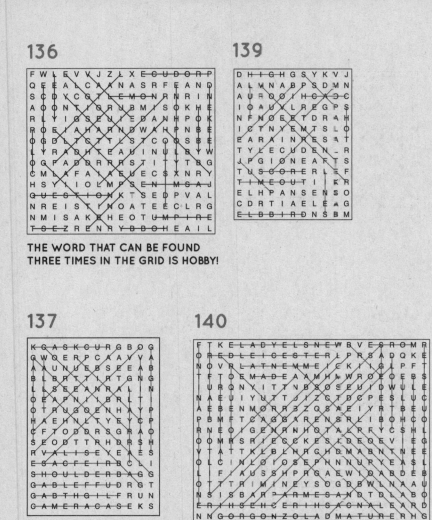

THE WORD THAT CAN BE FOUND THREE TIMES IN THE GRID IS HOBBY!

139

142

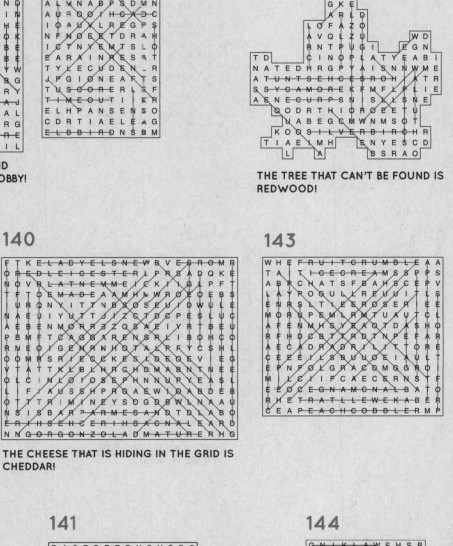

THE TREE THAT CAN'T BE FOUND IS REDWOOD!

137

WHY COULDN'T THE ELEPHANTS GO SWIMMING? BECAUSE THEY FORGOT THEIR TRUNKS!

140

THE CHEESE THAT IS HIDING IN THE GRID IS CHEDDAR!

143

138

141

144

145

147

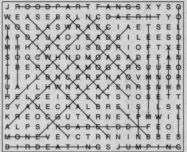

146

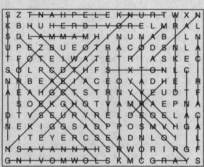

148

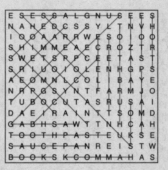

HOW DID YOU FIND THE
WEATHER AT CAMP?
EASY. I WENT OUTSIDE AND
THERE IT WAS!